The Findlater Sisters

The Findlater Sisters

LITERATURE & FRIENDSHIP

Eileen Mackenzie

JOHN MURRAY

Printed in Great Britain for
John Murray, Albemarle Street, London, by
Cox & Wyman Ltd., London, Fakenham,
and Reading

Contents

	Introduction	xi
1	Childhood at Lochearnhead	1
2	Prestonpans, First Novels	27
3	American Tour	49
4	Friendships Old and New	79
5	1914–1923	99
6	Rye and Comrie	116
7	Novels and Stories	128
	Books	146
	Index	147

Illustrations

Jane Findlater in her early twenties   *f.p.* 18

Mary Findlater in her early thirties   18

Mary and Jane 'novelists of repute'   82

Jane and Mary. *A drawing by Lady Jane Lindsay*   114

Jane and Mary at The House of Ross, Comrie, Perthshire   122

Jane and Mary at Earn Hope, Comrie, Perthshire   122

Acknowledgements

For permission to quote from copyright letters I wish to thank the following: Irene Helen, Lady Graves; The Earl of Crawford and Balcarres; Mr. Charles Gladstone; Mr. Leonard Woolf; Mr. John James; Mr. Richard de la Mare; Mrs. S. Benson and Mr. W. L. D'Arcy Hart.

I would also like to express my gratitude to my publisher Sir John Murray who, for his knowledge of and friendship for the Findlater sisters and many of their circle, has helped both with his interest and advice.

Introduction

The sisters, Mary and Jane Findlater, were Scottish novelists who in their day delighted with their books a wide public, which extended from the simplest folk to some of the highest in the land. What captivated the mass of readers, charmed also Prime Minister Gladstone, Archbishop Lang, Ellen Terry and Henry James, to name only a few of their distinguished admirers.

It was with Jane's first novel, *The Green Graves of Balgowrie*, published in 1896, that a literary name was made for both sisters. After this their books appeared almost biennially at first, and then at rather wider intervals. Whether they wrote separately or in partnership, fame and favour increased. In 1923 they wrote together and published their last book of any consequence, *Beneath the Visiting Moon*.

During the mid-nineteen twenties, almost as suddenly as it had arisen, their star declined. In the wider ranges of literature their quiet leisurely tones were drowned by harsher, more eccentric voices, while in their own line other Scottish novelists, who supplied pinker sugar than the Findlaters, or dwelt on darker crimes behind green shutters, were preferred.

The sisters accepted the change without rancour. They were passionately interested in the 'contemporary', its scientific developments, its thought, its art and, above all, in what they called their 'trade'. 'The present age must make its own books' they replied, when admirers begged them to produce another novel, and gracefully they retired from the literary stage, but remained as keen spectators of the drama of life and literature, 'assistantes' in the full sense.

In old age they liked to know that some readers still enjoyed their books, but they set no great store upon the survival of their novels after a generation or so. They had taken their art seriously and given of their best at the time, but this was an uneven best, fluctuating quite obviously on occasion because of ill health or direful circumstances, when a book had to be produced to keep the household going.

At its finest their art deserves something better than oblivion and Scotland, surely, would not wish hastily to forget two such distinguished daughters, writers who have a claim to be remembered whenever the history of the Scottish novel is brought up to date. Further, they were ladies of the old school. This is now a type little sought after, but the Findlaters were no conventional models. Fine and sensitive in feature and manner, apt of speech, brimming with intelligence, they possessed also the strong individuality and idiosyncrasy that have often flourished in the corners of Scotland and Ireland.

Even for an age which has provided for itself attractions more glamorous or more intriguingly complex, such personalities are worth a glance back, for a rare and refreshing quality lingers about them still, and may yet be discerned in their stories, by those who have an inclination to read.

This sketch of the sisters owes much to the impressions of their lifelong friends and something to my own early slight acquaintance with them and to my close contact of the last ten years with Mary Findlater herself who possessed a prodigious memory and an astonishing power of re-creating the past in conversational narrative. Further, it derives partly from my unpublished longer and fully documented account of them, the sources of which were:

1. Their father's diary, kept through the early years of his Ministry which began during the upheaval of the Disruption (1843)[1] and contained some recollections of his childhood.

---

[1] A schism which lasted until 1929. The strife orginated from the infringement of popular rights by the Patronage Act (1712). Nearly a third of the ministers and members of the Established Church of Scotland seceded to form the Free Church of Scotland.

2. Memories of various dates, set down from time to time by their mother.

3. Scattered letters from a store of interesting correspondence otherwise perished or lost through one and another vicissitude.

4. A sheaf of letters from Mary Findlater to her friend Marion Cadell of Cockenzie.

5. Two diaries of Mary Findlater's. In one of these she had summarized events contained in her own and Jane's original diaries, which after this were all destroyed, except for one kept by Mary during an American tour.

1

Childhood at Lochearnhead

When Mary and Jane Findlater, as young women, went to buy shoes in London, the fitter looked doubtfully at their exceedingly slim feet. He explained that the proportions were unusual, 'If you will forgive my saying so, ladies, they are old-fashioned, aristocratic feet.'

In truth, the sisters might well have belonged to a generation or two earlier than their contemporaries in age, for their parents did not marry until late in life, when they were quite old enough to have been the two girls' grandparents.

Their father, Eric Findlater, who was Minister of the Free Church at Lochearnhead, came from Durness, in the far north of Sutherland. Their mother was a Miss Borthwick of Edinburgh. The pair came from backgrounds widely discrepant. Yet Durness was not simply an outpost near Cape Wrath. Culdee missionaries had left ineradicable traces of civilization there. Robb Donn ('the Burns of Sutherland') whose songs and satires were known throughout the countryside, had lived there. It was a neighbourhood where gifted and eccentric characters flourished. The Reformation lairds, chiefs of the clan Mackay, who took over the Bishop's mansion at Balnakiel were in the van of the new movement. They chose ministers of parts and learning, thus setting a tradition for their descendants. Not least in the line at the manse was Mr. William Findlater who came of clerical forbears, natives in the late seventeenth century of Lanarkshire and Peebleshire.

Durness had its seasons, festivals and celebrations in which the Minister and the manse formed the centre and pivot. The family, of which Eric Findlater was the eldest, filled the roomy old house set in the spacious glebe which contained Mr. Findlater's carefully walled and much cherished garden. Dancing was sternly suppressed, but there were many other active and more venturous ploys, notably shinty played on Balnakiel strand. Music escaped condemnation. Mrs. William Findlater sang the wild Gaelic songs of the north with her children and husband around her, while a daughter, Jessie or Helen, one of the Findlater aunts of Mary's and Jane's childhood, accompanied on the piano.

Mrs. Findlater, daughter of Mr. John Thomson, whom William Findlater had succeeded as minister of Durness, was a beautiful woman and in her particular way, certainly a character. Stories and gossip accumulated about her. The poor loved her for her generosity. Going one better than St. Martin of Tours, she had given her whole cloak away to a shivering mortal on a bitterly cold day. Her own family dreaded her fierce, ungovernable temper, but she staunchly suffered privations and trials with her husband and children when the Disruption ousted them from her old home.

This upheaval touched comparatively gently the Borthwicks of Edinburgh. They agreed to differ when necessary, but cheerfully attended a church of 'the opposite camp' if filial duty and affection so demanded, nor was their admiration for a great preacher warped by partisan bias. Sarah Borthwick, who was to become the mother of the two authoresses, belonged like Eric Findlater to a numerous family. It was, however, largely composed of daughters and provided eight maiden aunts for Mary and Jane. As the Findlater sisters grew up, they sometimes regretted the young Borthwick uncle who died in his teens and might have had the romantic distinction of being a candidate for one of the oldest titles in Scotland.[1] Indeed, they could have wished for a benevo-

[1] The Borthwicks were an ancient family, reputed to have come to Scotland originally from Hungary, in the train of Margaret who married Malcolm Canmore, King of Scotland. This tradition is not accepted by all authorities, but it serves to represent the undeniable antiquity of the family. Burke's Peerage takes the title back to Sir William Borthwick, Keeper of Edinburgh Castle, who was granted permission by James of Scotland to built and fortify a castle in the Mote of Lochorwort. Sir William was made a Lord of Parliament as Lord Borthwick in 1452. The title became dormant more than once. It was taken by Cunninghame Borthwick a cousin of the Findlaters' young uncle Archibald Borthwick. Cunninghame's son Archibald, who became 17th Lord Borthwick, left no heir.

lent fairy to change at least some of that tribe of aunts into indulgent uncles.

The Borthwicks and especially Sarah, or Sally, as she was called had the genius for friendship and seemed to attract people of many types, especially those who had undergone strange or interesting experiences. They also loved to tell stories as a form of entertainment. Moreover, Sarah, along with her elder sister Jane, was gifted linguistically and both made translating from the German a special study.[1]

It was at the home of mutual friends, the Macgillivrays (Alexander Macgillivray,[2] son of the Minister of Lairg, had been Eric Findlater's companion and intimate since boyhood) that Sarah Borthwick often met her future husband, and liking ripened to love. He was forty-eight, she was thirty-eight when they married and the couple certainly provided an instance of being 'old enough to know their own minds'.

The marriage was an exceedingly happy one. There was deep, lasting affection on both sides, and mutual trust. Different backgrounds, complementary temperaments, tastes and friendships in common, together with love of the things of the mind, helped to secure the bond. The two were one in religious beliefs, and each possessed sufficient detachment from this world's goods to mitigate a life of comparative poverty, which was generally the lot of a Free Church minister and his family.

That perfect relationship between the parents was a corner stone in the lives of their children to whom it gave a deep sense of security. This Mary and Jane took for granted from their earliest years, but remembered with gratitude in maturity.

Mr. and Mrs. Findlater were not young when they married and, as they put it, 'had scarcely expected the blessing of children'. But children there were; a son who died at birth and three daughters, the eldest of whom was born at Lochearnhead on 9th August,

---

[1] Some of their hymn translations are still used. Sarah contributed 53 of the 122 hymns in Jane Borthwick's best known collection (1854) v. p. 20

[2] The Rev. Alexander Macgillivray, Free Church Minister.

1862, and christened Sarah Jemima. She was always known as Mora (the Gaelic version of Sarah) and just as several years separated her from her two younger sisters, so her interests and rather unhappy temperament differed from theirs.

The elder of the two authoresses was born at the manse on 28th March, 1865, and named Mary Williamina. The youngest of the family, Jane Helen Findlater, was born just over a year and a half after her sister Mary, on 4th November, 1866. Her mother was staying in Edinburgh with her family at 14 Claremont Crescent, at the time of the baby's birth. This was a house which became very familiar to the girls in subsequent years when they stayed there as not very happy guests of their Borthwick aunts.

Mrs. Findlater was attached especially to Mora. Mr. Findlater's favourite was Jane, but Mary declared that her parents were far too just, fair and affectionate to all three children to make her feel neglected or the 'odd man out', so that she was never conscious of any inequality of affection, and was completely satisfied from childhood to old age, with the steadfast love of her sister Jane.

Their devotion to each other began in early childhood. Mary loved Jane as far back as she could remember, which was the day when she saw her sister's little bonnet and cloak laid out upon a bed in the nursery, in readiness for her christening.

Jane's nature was so exquisitely gentle and sympathetic that as she grew up she was loved by all who knew and surrounded her, even by the difficult Mora, and above all by Mary, who described their relationship as 'halves of one whole'. When Mary, as a child, was distressed or weeping, Jane in an abandonment of sympathy would offer all her treasured possessions to comfort her, including the most precious of all, a primitively carved Eskimo doll. Each night she prayed fervently for this doll, among her family petitions, until she was forbidden to do so, a prohibition which puzzled her tender heart. Indeed the ways of Providence had early seemed inscrutable to her. She prayed constantly and earnestly for a pony, but always in vain.

Mary, though possessed of a happy enough temperament was far more tempestuous by nature than her younger sister. On one occasion when she had been put to bed for some misdemeanour, her fierce little teeth bit through the sheet. Even her love for Jane was once drowned in an access of jealousy during a children's party at Edenchip. Their hostess Lady Helen Macgregor, had given each child a present. Jane received a pair of exquisite little red shoes with tasselled ties. Mary's present was a quite ordinary child's toy, in the form of some animal. She hated it and longed for red shoes. Retreating under the table, a favourite refuge of hers, she gnawed and destroyed the unwanted gift, while she watched the red shoes bobbing about on Jane's happy small feet.

After one particular outburst, the rages were cured permanently, for she caught sight of her father's stricken expression, as he groaned, 'That child has got her grandmother's temper!' Somehow the little girl grasped the portent of this remark. It made such a deep impression upon her that she never allowed wild fury to carry her away again.

Mary and Jane seldom played in the garden. They preferred a spot just outside, beneath an old oak tree on a mound, carpeted with moss and fine, soft grass. Not far off was the great 'standing stone', a monolith which seemed to peer over the garden wall, and there were various large grey stones scattered about in the bright, long grass. On the hillside that rose opposite, behind the manse, were the larger stones of a Pictish village. This was rather beyond the children's range, and there were other attractions nearer home. One day, sitting before a large hole, framed by tree roots and sheltered by greenery, a great 'black and white cat' appeared. In a moment Mary knew that it was a badger and called Jane to look at this entrancing and exciting creature. Jane, who thought it was a lovely cat, specially come to make their acquaintance, was sadly disappointed, when, in a flash, the creature vanished, never to be seen by the children again.

Farther afield, near the entrance to Edenchip, the home of the Macgregors, the little girls used to play around a small pool with a strange white surface. Sometimes they would bring back the water in a cup or bottle, pretending it was precious medicine prescribed for some imaginary patient, sick doll or animal, or they would simply watch the oily element (for such apparently, it was) separate itself fascinatingly in the liquid.

During the long winter months, indoor playgrounds had to be substituted for outdoor which were sopping wet or buried in moist snow. The nursery, papered with innumerable pictures, mostly black and white, presented a scrap-book of never-ending interest to the children's eyes. Under the table was also a favourite haunt. Here there were almost unlimited possibilities of cave-dwelling, playing at houses, being on board ship or living in an ark. Sometimes, under the protective roof of the table top, Mary and Jane would sit looking at picture-books. Puzzled by some illustration one day, Mary crawled out and taking the book to her mother, begged, 'Tell me about it.' Smiling, her mother looked up from her own book. 'Child, child,' she exclaimed, 'it's time you learnt to read for yourself!' The little girl returned to her refuge under the table to begin the struggle by which she taught herself, mostly by independent efforts, to read and 'find out' for herself.

It was an isolated and lonely life in winter for the children at the manse. In summer there were comings and goings, but even then it was something of an event when another small girl appeared. A missionary friend of their mother's had brought the children a number of large, brightly coloured, exotic feathers. They were admiring the brilliant shades, feeling the soft tendrils against their cheeks, or joyfully waving the gay, dancing plumes, when the maid announced, 'Mrs. Hill'. A lady, who appeared to fill the doorway with her large presence, was ushered in. Beside her walked a small person of about four years old, her stepdaughter, still clad in semi-mourning for her mother, who had died more than a year previously.

The children eyed one another shyly. Little Margaret Hill was given one of the bright, graceful feathers for her own, and the grown-ups soon became involved in talk among themselves. Before long the children were playing together. It was the beginning of a lifetime's friendship. After this, Margaret was often at the manse and the girls became playmates during the

Hills' stay at Lochearnhead and for many subsequent summer visits, for Mr. Hill[1] built a house within walking distance of the manse.

Margaret was a rather grave, self-contained little person, but although her mother had died when she was three, just when the child would miss her devastatingly, she did not mope persistently, nor did she resent her rather absurd step-mother. Mr. Hill had married again speedily as much for his young daughter's sake as for his own. Time endorsed this step, unromantic though it may have been. In another family disaster or tragedy might have followed, but given the Hills' innate good sense and balanced temperaments, the result was happy. Margaret gained a careful, affectionate guardian, and her father, a devoted housekeeper who looked after and cherished him, especially through the severe and testing Scottish winters. 'Mr. Hill', his wife would remark with an air of supreme satisfaction, 'is *composed* of flannel!'

The high spirits which underlay Margaret's sedate exterior and her talent for mimicry never tempted her to take advantage where it would have been so easy. She was, and remained always, the soul of discretion and loyalty. Her cheerful, equable, independent disposition made her a strength and stay to the Findlater sisters for a lifetime. Where they were highly sensitive, swept by moods, and from their very gifts, liable to be influenced, sometimes depressed, by external pressures or atmosphere, she seemed fortified and immune.

Mary and Jane never forgot Margaret's youthful observation, that if they waited for someone to come and make them happy they might wait for ever. Happiness, according to her, was one's own inner concern. She certainly lived up to this precept unfailingly through her student period, when she read classics at Dundee University and later as minister's wife at Wick.[2]

Even that remote, and in her younger days, unprepossessing, grim small town did not daunt her. She was keenly interested in

---

[1] The Rev. Thomas Hill, Free Church Minister.

[2] Margaret Hill married in 1890 Nigel Roberton, Free Church Minister, Wick.

the people and their lives. They took the place of the children she would have liked to have, but for whom she never permitted herself to repine. She was recompensed by the filial devotion of a whole neighbourhood.

Time passes slowly for children. Now and then at Lochearnhead, it seemed scarcely to move at all. One day was so like another. 'Nothing ever happens here,' said Mary and Jane. In fact many things were happening. Mora was growing up into a very pretty, rather unhappy girl, and the younger sisters were registering much that they were to rediscover, stored in their memories in later life.

> . . . perhaps there is no more compelling force than just these heavy, ordinary years that pass over us one by one. We think ourselves the same, and at the end of the time we are really altogether different.[1]

Doubtless their youthful existence was shielded and, on the whole unexciting, but there were thrills and horrors to be had, even within the sober precincts of the manse.

There was an occasion, when, as dusk fell, Mary and Jane, who had gone to bed, espied from their window the elders in solemn procession arriving at the gate. They had come to see the minister and the children felt the tension and gravity of the occasion, although they did not know fully for many years afterwards what it was all about. There was indeed serious trouble, for evil goings-on had been discovered at the local inn and the elders had come to ask the minister to excommunicate the innkeeper. After this disciplinary action had been taken, the girls used to listen with shocked fascination to the curses called down on the minister and the manse by the miscreant's carter (under instructions from his master) every time he passed the manse gates.

Out in the kitchen, Mary and Jane could get their 'thrillers' and enjoy them at an age earlier than even many modern children. Mrs. King, the cook, was a gifted horror-monger, and the girls were enthralled by the murder stories which she told with gusto

---

[1] *Penny Monypenny*, London, 1912, p. 89.

and a certain command of language. But one day as Mrs. King was carrying a dish into the dining-room, she staggered and lurched against the sideboard. 'Oh, Mrs. King, are you ill?' anxiously exclaimed Mrs. Findlater. The girls could hear their father's quiet undertone from the other end of the table, 'She's drunk!' After that Mrs. King was sent away. Mary and Jane alone regretted her departure.

Another woman made life a burden to the household by her mad temper and intractable moods. Poor Mrs. Findlater felt that the situation was getting beyond her when Aunt Jessie arrived on a visit. Hearing of their trouble and how at that very moment cook was indulging in one of her fits of anger in the kitchen, Aunt Jessie drew herself up. 'Let me see to this', said she, 'I rather like a tussle.' Thankful to leave to her sister-in-law's generalship the battle which was so distasteful to her, Mrs. Findlater withdrew. The two small girls followed at a safe distance as their aunt proceeded, to their surprise, without a tremor, in the direction of danger.

As she entered the kitchen, the cook, her back turned towards the door, was giving vent to her fury in hurling a few utensils to the floor. Aunt Jessie stood for a moment, very upright, beside the kitchen table, then she rapped sharply upon it twice. 'Come, come, come!' she exclaimed, in tones of mingled sternness and command. The woman swung round, but either the shock of the unexpected voice, or something compelling about the presence of Aunt Jessie, perhaps both, took immediate effect. In a matter of seconds, cook was reasonably calm and tractable. With some more of Aunt Jessie's admonitions and her influence in the house for several weeks, the cure was completed, and worked for a considerable time.

Mrs. Findlater concerned herself to a great extent with the welfare in body, mind and spirit of the people of Lochearnhead. She inaugurated a coffee-house and library there and did much to eliminate drinking habits from the neighbourhood. Her daughters could remember a time when almost every second man on the road appeared to be drunk. The complete change came about during the comparatively short space of their youth at Locheárn-head.

Their mother believed it to be part of their education to know something of the lives of the people around them, and she also endeavoured to give them object lessons in the circumstances and fate of those who seemed to have reaped their appropriate reward. The film experiences of some modern children could scarcely be more dubious than those of Mary and Jane Findlater, who were taken as small girls, to witness the death-bed of a pious villager, so that they might see how a Christian should die, in serene confidence. An effective contrast and warning was provided for the young people in the harrowing state of 'Black John', a village evil-doer, in his last tortured hours. These death-bed scenes did not, however, create the impression that their mother desired for her children. Mary and Jane were too young and too sensitive to feel in either instance anything other than revulsion. At a slightly more advanced age they could give (for Mary and Jane often thought and felt together) no stock Christian comfort, but simply a swift human response to a young life fearful of extinction. Annie Ferguson, a village girl, was untouched by the pious hopes and conventional beliefs offered to her. She was young. She did not want to die. As Mary and Jane, following their mother, turned to leave the cottage, the poor girl, with a desperate gesture, caught at Mary's hand. The terror written on her young, worn face was so heart-rending, that Mary could find no words as she looked down at her. She found them afterwards in a poem.[1]

Mercifully there were other more cheerful processes of education. The three girls had a series of governesses, who seem to have been of a happier breed than was very usual in days when these often unfortunate women might so easily possess the traits of a hated and down-trodden race, bullying their charges and cringing before their employers.

The first of her line at the manse was Miss Annie Lorrain Smith. She was a remarkable woman, who afterwards became a

[1] *Songs and Sonnets,* London, 1895, pp. 13–14.

distinguished botanist.[1] She did not imbue her pupils with any special liking for this subject but, perhaps, more to her credit, she gave them invaluable stimulus, for she possessed the independent, questioning attitude of the really thoughtful mind. This she encouraged in her pupils. They were to find out for themselves, to struggle towards their own ideas and conclusions. Miss Lorrain Smith was plain, forthright, even a little uncouth. But there was nothing uncouth about her mentality. It had characteristics which in those days would have been considered 'masculine'. The type was, perhaps, less uncommon among Scottish women, where it went with great individuality. With her Mary and Jane came to their first realization of Shakespeare. She read *Julius Caesar* to them, expounding a little, but mainly, through her interpretive reading, allowing the play to speak for itself. That night Mary could not sleep for excitement and crept downstairs after lights were out, so as to read by her candle, once more, the haunting, magical words of Mark Antony's great speech over the dead Caesar.

Education was not restricted to object lessons in the village of living and dying, holy or unholy, nor to the teaching of governesses. Mr. and Mrs. Findlater's closest friends were always interesting. More than all others, 'Uncle Mac' (their father's friend Alexander Macgillivray) drew Mary and Jane like a magnet. With his Highland second sight, his wonderful stories, literary learning and quick emotions, he had much to give to these highly intelligent, sensitive girls. When they were children he used to take the small pair on his knee and repeat long passages to them from Shakespeare, Milton or Wordsworth, especially from *The Prelude*.

---

[1] Dr. J. Ramsbottom kindly supplied information about Miss Annie Lorrain Smith of which the following is a summary.

She was born at Halfmerton, Dumfrieshire 23rd October, 1854, and came of a family with a fine scholastic record. She studied in France and Germany and took posts as a governess until about 1888, when she went to the Royal College of Science. She became an authority on seaweeds, fungi and lichens, wrote learned works held important posts and became one of the original women members of the Linnean Society, serving also on its Council. President of the British Mycological Society 1907 and 1922. A woman of wide interests and an ardent suffragette. Died 1937.

"You won't understand this now,' he would say, 'but one day you will remember it'. They listened uncomprehendingly, yet spellbound by the sound of the words.

They did not weary of listening to this kind of thing, but hundreds of sermons fell upon their voluntarily or involuntarily deaf ears, and were consigned to oblivion as soon as possible, together with the weary services, which they sat through Sunday after Sunday. One sermon alone stood out in their memories. It was preached by the magic tongue of 'Uncle Mac', about the Walk to Emmaus. Two of his congregation, at least, felt that they had trodden the road themselves, the memory was not of a sermon, but of an experience.

Until the days when Mary and Jane became personally acquainted with the great preachers of their time, this state of affairs was exceptional. Their father was a remote person to the sisters and they probably knew the general tenor of his sermons too well to pay great heed to them, even after they were of an age to understand them. Eric Findlater's years made him appear to his children as at two stages removed, more like a grandfather than a father. He seemed to them a kindly, benevolent figure, but in the background, living a life far distant from theirs. He was much shut away in his study, reading, writing, brooding, smoking a pipe and conversing with his friends, who from time to time visited the manse. Despite slender means he was always elegantly dressed and wore shoes which were specially made for him in beautiful, brown leather, a colour not usual for a cleric of his day, and which drew attention to the fine shape of his feet. With his tall, slim figure, greying dark hair and beard, his swarthy, handsome features his appearance was impressive and interesting. The winning blend of dignity and friendliness in his manner captured the hearts of nearly all who approached him and made him beloved among his parishioners.

The elderly minister could enter very little into his children's lives, except through one channel. If his sermons never reached them, he could hold their attention by his way of bringing to life an incident from the Bible. He would give to his version of the story imaginative touches of realism for their benefit, until his more matter-of-fact little wife would look up with a smiling reproof at her husband, for 'adding something' that was 'not actually in the text of Holy Writ'.

Their father's study was sacrosanct and the children were not supposed to enter it unannounced. For this reason, and also because it was at the back of the house, off the beaten track of their normal comings and goings, they comparatively seldom crossed the threshold. Once, however, Mary, bent on some purpose of her own, and supposing that her father was out, entered the study without knocking. No sooner had she done so than she stood stock still. Her father was there, kneeling, absorbed in prayer. So wrapt was he, that she sensed his complete unawareness of his material surroundings or of her presence. In a moment she crept away, ashamed of her intrusion and awed, beyond the utterance of a child's tongue, by the Presence she had felt in that room. It was something she had never experienced in the little church they attended every Sunday.

There the services were long and wearisome for a child, and they were part of a never-ending, imprisoning Sunday, when reading, walking, music, painting and all the pleasing activities of the week, mental or physical, were restricted or forbidden. In some ways, to sit or stand in the little, bare church, with its narrow unstained wooden seats and the clear windows looking out on the surrounding birch trees, must have been a relief, though not one which was greatly appreciated by the sisters. Mary, for reasons, doubtless, psychological rather than purely physical, produced a faint or two, which protected her subsequently from endless standing, though not from actual church attendance. As the girls' eyes wandered to the windows where they could watch in spring or summer the sunlight dance on the rippling festoons of soft green birch leaves, they would muse a little, questioning even in their childish minds the sober melancholy of the congregation as the members sadly and solemnly admonished each other to 'serve Him with mirth' and rejoice.

Yet despite gloom and restrictions, Mary and Jane had one

another, and increasingly their companionship grew from an unconscious to a conscious necessity. They felt alike, they thought alike, but mutually brought all the joy of the responsive 'other' mind. Even at this early age there were similarities in appearance and unity in thought, yet as Lady Grey[1] once remarked 'they tasted different.'

All three sisters inherited their father's dark good looks, not the fair skins of the Borthwicks or of Aunt Jessie Findlater. A broad low forehead gave to Mora a cast of countenance rather unlike that of her two younger sisters. The faces of Mary and Jane were markedly more intellectual than hers. Mary's exquisitely cut, small aquiline features, quick, rather piercing dark eyes, finely traced brows and uncontrollable masses of almost black hair, Jane's beautifully shaped dark head, with features also aquiline, though less strictly handsome, possessed a distinction which could have made a passer-by look at them twice. In her youthful photographs, the sensitive line of Jane's mouth and the setting of her finely shaped eyes are impressive, though no photograph could convey the real loveliness of her eyes.

A correspondent who knew them then wrote to the sisters years after, recalling his youthful admiration, 'Those days are stamped on my memory for ever; are there any girls as beautiful now as you were?'[2]

These two faces were not of the type one would ordinarily expect to see in a Scottish manse. Intellect might flourish there sometimes and good looks, but the features and colouring of these girls suggested far other skies, far other seas, and the ancient culture of the Mediterranean.

The pair whose lives were so closely and intimately linked were parted only for limited periods during their eighty years together. For them separation, the inevitability of separation, was the Shadow of Shadows. It was something encountered only twice

[1] Dorothy Widdrington, who became Sir Edward Grey's first wife.

[2] Quoted jokingly in a letter from Jane to Marion Cadell. The name of the admirer is not mentioned. The letter which is dated only 'Sunday evening' seems to belong to 1932 or 1933.

in their lives as a Presence, before death took one of them, and it seems as if the earliest experience of this terror, which seized them first in childhood, was not recognized by them for what it was, until they knew it for the second time as grown women.

The first strange encounter took place at Lochearnhead on a smiling summer's afternoon. They were out with Mora and their governess, then the pretty Miss Jane Robertson, and the four were descending a hillside a little beyond Edenchip. Mary and Jane were, as usual, together, while the other two had drawn slightly ahead. Before long, since the small girls' legs were shorter and because the afternoon was so pleasant that they were inclined to loiter, Mora and her companion had disappeared, but Mary and Jane knew their way, and happy as always in each other's company, proceeded along their path without a thought of danger or distress. Then suddenly, unaccountably and simultaneously, the whole day seemed to darken and Fear rose, like a great sinister force. It was so tangible and inescapable that they used to wonder in more mature years, when they looked back upon the episode, whether indeed some dreadful thing had been done upon those slopes, a deed so evil and violent that the reverberations roll over the hillside from time to time with fearful iteration. When, however, this terror and misery assailed them as grown women, they recognized, or thought they knew its origin.

As panic seized the two small girls that afternoon, they began to run. They never ceased running until they came up beside their sister and governess, who had noticed nothing at all.

This occasion was far more alarming to them than a night of fear which was engraved clearly enough upon their minds, but during which they were within the strong walls of the manse and in the reassuring vicinity of their parents. This was a night towards the end of December 1879[1] long remembered not only by the two girls who could not sleep for the noise and fury of the storm, but by all those who awoke the next day to hear before many hours had elapsed the heavy news of the Tay Bridge disaster.

[1] 28th December, 1879.

Some of the villagers at Lochearnhead thought that the end of the world had come that night. Above the roar of the wind and the crackle and boom of thunder a wild voice was heard from someone running frantically around the manse, crying, 'Let me in, let me in, it's the Judgement Day!' This was poor lonely Mary Fisher (who had once abruptly left her laundry work at the manse in tears, because a chicken had been slaughtered there that day) and no sooner had she been admitted when close on her heels followed two other villagers, Kate Parlance and Black John, the local reprobate, neither of whom expected their frail cottages to withstand the storm. All three were determined to be close to their revered Minister, if it were indeed the Crack of Doom. The refugees joined the household around the kitchen fire and were comforted by a substantial tea.

As well as terrors and excitements, life at Lochearnhead had its idyllic moments. Some of these are described in the sisters' novel *Penny Monypenny*, for instance, the coming of spring. In the Highlands it seemed more than merely a change of season, for it came out of the desolate, dripping caverns of winter, with the brilliant triumph of resurrection.[1] Or later, in summer the air would sparkle on

a clear hot day that follows the track of grey weather.

Then the whole countryside would seem

adorned – every roadside hung with bells and ferns; the little burns twisting and glancing from under the long grasses that overhung their course like eyelashes over bright eyes; the short turf upon the mountain slopes was starred with infinitely small yellow and purple flowers, the birch trees stood like nymphs arrested in a dance – even the boggy ground about them was full of soft hues, like some faintly coloured Eastern carpet; a scent of spice and honey filled the air, and the sky was without a cloud.[2]

[1] *Penny Monypenny,* London, 1912, p. 14.
[2] Ibid., p. 159.

Enchanted times there were. 'Green Apple Days', the Findlater sisters and their intimates called them, because on one superb summer morning Charlotte Stewart,[1] Margaret Hill, Mary and Jane had gone off together, and everything, down to the smallest detail had turned out perfectly. Between them all they had only a few green apples for sustenance, but it was one of those magic days when nothing could go wrong and happiness overflowed, so that for ever after, even a paler reflection of this experience was called among them 'a green apple day'.

Remembered joy, delightful associations are cumulative and possess their own special charm, in layer upon precious layer, but nothing, Mary and Jane considered could quite equal again the first fine youthful rapture, because for a full response to the spell of summer and to the 'top of the morning', one must be young. Mary would sometimes recall that particular and incomparable ecstasy of looking out of her bedroom window at the manse, on a perfect summer morning when the Grass of Parnassus which spread its creamy whiteness over the ground on the opposite side of the road, was not stirred by the slightest ripple of wind, and the name which always charmed her ear, sounded its soft sibilant notes, held eternally and long drawn out in that bright morning calm.

Such experiences were of inestimable value, but they were rare. More often existence at Lochearnhead was dreary and cramping, especially throughout the long winter months. As daughters of the manse and nieces of a bevy of Victorian aunts, restrictions and standards of behaviour must have been shackling and frequently galling to young, high spirited, intelligent girls. Their parents' friends, however dear and interesting, belonged, after all, to an elder day and there were long periods of isolation from their own contemporaries.

At sixteen and seventeen respectively, Jane and Mary attended a winter school in Edinburgh, but they were unhappy, felt that they were learning little and came home to a spring and summer beclouded by a sense of having nothing to do. Worse misery

[1] Charlotte Stewart of Ardvorlich.

followed when the sisters were parted for some months during which Jane was dangerously ill in Edinburgh. But it was at this time that Mary and Charlotte Stewart of Ardvorlich made friends and in the following spring and summer, when Jane was back again and well, the three became inseparable companions. Jane felt as if a new world had opened for Mary and herself. The girls had tastes and talents in common. Charlotte Stewart, like the Findlaters, was to become a novelist. Later, under the name of Allan McAulay, she wrote Scottish historical romances. She was passionately interested in history as the Findlaters never were and wrote books which involved respectively a considerable study of Robert Burns[1] and of Napoleon[2] to whom, Mary considered, she bore a curious facial resemblance. Her youthful photograph portrays a handsome, rather broad oval face, with clear cut features. She was dark and pale, with a liveliness and vivacity inherited from some Greek ancestry. Before her vitality burnt itself out, she possessed physical strength and energy which far surpassed those of Mary and Jane.

Together, Charlotte, Mary and Jane, used to write stories, though the Findlaters' first attempts went back to a date far earlier than this. Mary used to say, 'I can't remember when we *began* to write, we were always writing.'

From childhood the two girls had listened to Mrs. Findlater's inexhaustible fund of stories, long and short, most of them actual happenings, many of which were used later for their books. Now, Mrs. Stewart, Charlotte's mother, sometimes joined the three girls, bringing a further range of experience and wisdom from half a lifetime in India and her travels as an officer's wife.

Mrs. Stewart, though an apparently aloof and distant person, was loved, especially by young people, and by her servants. She spoke seldom, but Mary and Jane came to realize that when she did so, her advice, as they put it 'was worth more than a lawyer's fee'. She drew neither from book-learning, nor from mere travel, but from her own, much pondered and considered interpretation of life, which was deeply tinged with tragedy.

[1] *The Rhymer*, 1900.   [2] *The Eagle's Nest*, 1910.

Mary Findlater in her early thirties

Jane Findlater in her early twenties

Thus Mary's and Jane's minds were stored with tales from far and wide, from the distant past but, yet more, from 'fifty years since', within the cognisance of their parents' generation. They received what was living yet in living memory and re-lived it in their vivid, young imaginations. During the apparently eventless days and more especially in the winter, when bad weather often prevented other activities, reading and story telling were the chief pastimes. There was no lack of books at the manse, and the newer ones would come on loan from Mr. Findlater's friends or in a large bundle from Edinburgh. Moreover, in both the Findlater and Borthwick families, story telling seems to have been something of an art.

Aunts came and went unceasingly at Lochearnhead, or, it might be truer to say that they never really went. Often there was one staying at the manse, and the Miss Borthwicks built a house in the neighbourhood, above the entrance to Glen Ogle. There they took up residence during the summer.

The three aunts who survived from a family of nine sisters were full of missionary zeal and their not inconsiderable combined wealth was drained off, almost exclusively, in this one direction. Apparently, their watchful eyes failed to observe the crippling burden of poverty at the manse or the extent to which the nieces were weighed down and hampered by it.

What Aunt Jane did observe was a 'wayward girl', for this is how she often alluded to her niece Mary in the vast *Journal* where she recorded events and poured out her religious and other sentiments. On one occasion at Lochearnhead, she wrote, 'I too happened to be out late in the moonlight and came upon the romantic pair.'

Mary commented, 'i.e. "the wayward girl" and some young man equally "wayward".'

So old, so cold and so gruel-fed in mind and body was how Aunt Jane appeared to her nieces then, and it was only years afterwards that they realized the blindness on their side, for the older woman was really carrying on what she would have described as 'spiritual warfare' and this 'of the most unremitting sort, against fears and despondency which she regarded as her besetting sin'.[1]

The aunts' charity was steadily directed abroad and consumed in efforts to convert 'the heathen'. Yet, from all accounts, the Miss Borthwicks were pleasant kindly people, if limited in outlook, precise to primness and somewhat censorious about their nieces. Beneath this surface their own struggles went on, almost entirely concealed from their young relatives.

Mary and Jane on their side were critical, especially of the intellectual powers of their aunts. These were, perhaps, greater than youthful judgement would admit. Aunt Jane, considerably the eldest, and the outstanding character among the sisters, read Jacob Boehme and possessed a most competent knowledge of German. A note in the *British Weekly* (22nd March, 1896) in connection with a review of Mary's books mentions that,

Miss Findlater's Aunt Miss Borthwick published the well-known *Hymns from the Land of Luther*.

'Miss Cameron' in Mary's book *A Narrow Way* is clearly sketched from the Borthwick aunts and outwardly, in her habits and tricks of speech, is Aunt Jane.

Did the Miss Borthwicks guess that the Findlater aunts were awarded higher marks for intellect by their precocious nieces? Native intelligence alone gained them the prize, for their education had been sketchy in the extreme. In no small part, this was the result of poverty which was visited upon the children, and many instances upon the grandchildren, of those ministers who sacrificed material security by 'coming out' in the Disruption. The situation is well illustrated in two generations of Findlaters.

Mary's heart warmed even to 'the black sheep' Aunt Robina Findlater who, beside her niece on a London bus, cried out, 'I may be poor, I may be old, but I'm *alive* in a wonderful world!'

Aunt Robina had to be forbidden the manse, but Aunt Helen

[1] The quotation from the *Journal* and the comments are from a letter from Mary Findlater to Marion Cadell, 25th April, 1916.

and Aunt Jessie were always welcome there and to their nieces. Aunt Jessie Findlater foresaw, long before the real difficulties came, how wrong things were likely to go with her niece Mora. 'Your mother,' she said to Mary and Jane, 'should recognize that Mora has not your intellectual interests. What she needs is to have some pretty clothes and to be taken out to parties.'

Pretty clothes, alas, did not come the way of any of the three, but here, lack of money was not the whole trouble. Their mother had no idea how to dress children. The girls were often quaintly garbed and soon they became painfully conscious of this. They wore polonaises and striped petticoats when these had become old-fashioned and odd. One day as Mary and Jane stood in a friendly porch to shelter from the rain, some passing children glancing their way, began to laugh. The truth dawned on the sisters, 'they're laughing at us!' they gasped, as they looked down at their anti-quated garments. 'Put on your prettiest frocks tonight,' commanded Mrs. Stewart on an occasion when the girls were staying at Ardvorlich, 'for I have a charming young man coming to dinner.'[1] Up went Mary and Jane to their bedroom and then, with tears, realized that they had no pretty frocks. But, philosophically, and encouraging one another, they pulled themselves together and went downstairs, resolved not to let clothes spoil the evening, and, indeed, their troubles were soon forgotten.

On a visit to other friends, their luggage was temporarily lost and they were lent evening dresses by their hostess's daughter. These seemed a delightful substitute for their own rather quaint garments, but poor Jane, who suffered from acute shyness, spilt coffee down the front of the lovely pink satin dress she had on. The evening would have been entirely ruined for her, had it not been for the kindly sympathy and attention of another guest, Dr. Joseph Bell,[2] who helped her to forget her embarrassment. He had already fascinated Mary's imagination by recognizing her as her father's daughter before he knew her name. She was by no means

[1] The future Sir Charles Heaton–Ellis.

[2] Joseph Bell, M.D., F.R.C.S. (Edin.), born 2nd December, 1837, d. 4th October, 1911.

a feminine replica of her father, but for Dr. Bell there were certain clear indications in her appearance from which he made his deduction. This habit of his was one which entertained and impressed his medical students and which he used to aid his diagnoses, with considerable skill. In Edinburgh he was a well-known figure as he drove his dogcart through the streets. Slim, dark with piercing grey eyes and aquiline nose, he was an impressive-looking person, this prototype of Sherlock Holmes.[1] From the moment of their first meeting Dr. Bell was a hero in the eyes of the sisters. For his part, from that day, he was their kind and devoted friend.

Mary maintained that as she and Jane grew up they were rather too much surrounded by women. Nevertheless, they were certainly not segregated. For several years, during the holidays two brothers, young de Wattevilles, came to the manse as a second home, and filled it with music and singing. The link with this Berne family[2] had been established by Aunt Jane Borthwick, who had a number of friends in Germany and Switzerland and was very interested in the Swiss Protestant Church.

With Walter de Watteville, who became a doctor, after studying at Edinburgh, Mary and Jane made a lasting friendship. None of the sisters was very musical, but they enjoyed hearing the de Wattevilles' songs and especially Walter's voice, which developed into a magnificent maturity. Jane could sing sweetly, but shyness prevented her ever performing much.

Other youthful friends were the Grays, who visited Lochearnhead for many summers. One fine, warm afternoon, Mrs. Findlater announced to her daughters that she was going to call on the Grays, who had taken a farm at Lochearnhead for some weeks. Mora succeeded in keeping out of the enterprise, Mary and Jane, half snobbishly, half in fun, declared that they had no wish to make the acquaintance of 'ironmongers', an attitude which curiously enough, was more in keeping with contemporary social

---

[1] Cp. Heskith Pearson, *Conan Doyle,* 1943, chap. VI.

[2] The von Wattenwyls or de Wattevilles were a patrician family who played an important part in the history of the city and republic of Berne. Several had connections with Great Britain.

conventions than their mother's determination to call. Mrs. Find-later, however, was firm, and the pair unwillingly accompanied her.

As they reached the house, two young men in white flannels, who had been sitting reading on a seat near the porch, sprang up to greet them. They took Mrs. Findlater into the house to see their mother and returned to entertain the girls, delighted to find that one of them was 'the most beautiful girl in the world'. Charles Gray had rushed home somewhile previously to inform his astonished family that he had seen this vision in the village shop.[1] Now he knew that she was Mary Findlater.

While the parents discoursed indoors, the four young people sat chatting outside. Active, interesting minds and good manners soon overcame all Mary's and Jane's prejudice, serious or other-wise. From that occasion dated a friendship with the whole Gray family, girls and boys, for the entire mortal span.

With the boys, as they grew into young men, Mary and Jane would discuss everything in heaven and earth. Especially with Herbert Gray[2] would they argue on theological matters. Charles used to try to explain to them what he felt was inherently different between the masculine and feminine point of view. In this way and at an early age, the two future authoresses came to know something of the masculine mind, which might have remained for much longer a closed book to them.

Miss Gertrude Gray, a sister of Charles and Herbert, remarked that she wondered how her brothers 'got by' such attractive and delightful girls as Mary and Jane Findlater. But the two were wrapped up in each other and though they were quite normal in their liking for and admiration of a fine young man, and ready for gay compliments and tokens of affection, the perfect soul's

---

[1] This incident was described to me by Charles Gray's sister, Miss Gertrude Gray.

[2] Dr. Herbert Gray 1868–1956, M.A. (Edin.) D.D. (Glasgow). Presby-terian Minister, son of Alexander Gray of Edinburgh. Married 1897 Mary Christian daughter of the Rev. Marcus Dods, D.D. Held a sequence of educa-tional and church posts in Edinburgh, Manchester and London. Author of numerous books on religious and social questions.

companionship between the sisters made other relationships seem commonplace or superflous.

Mrs. Stewart of Ardvorlich had warned Mary that it would be unwise to expect a relationship with the kindest husband to be as harmonious and perfect as that which existed between her and Jane. Mary became engaged for a brief time to a young man, 'I think,' so she remarked to me, 'merely because he was so handsome.' Suddenly, one day she realized that there would have to be a parting from Jane. She immediately broke off the engagement. There was grief on both sides. The poor young man was angry as well as hurt. He dramatically threw the engagement ring into the fire. Mary's woes, though acute enough, were short-lived. She was far too high-spirited to allow herself to be heartsick for long.

In this she was very different from Mora, whose whole life was overshadowed by an unhappy love affair. Jane, also, had her 'fancy,' but, mercifully, as it turned out, the affair came to nothing. As years went on, the two sisters used to say laughingly, '*We* could only marry a Mormon.' Certainly Mary's quick tongue and keen-edged sense of the ridiculous would have been somewhat daunting to potential lovers. The Gray family long treasured her observation to Gertrude on the news of her sister, Constance Gray's engagement, 'You and I, Gertie, will never get married, we talk too much. It's only those who sit like Connie silent and highly flushed.'

Life was not altogether dull at Lochearnhead, but lack of satisfying occupation was a recurrent fret. Marriage and the alternative of caring for elderly or youthful relatives, perhaps both, were the main employments for which the nineteenth-century woman could hope. Certainly the seven girls living near the northern shore of Loch Earn, the three Findlaters, Charlotte Stewart, and the three Macgregors of Edenchip, with their 'Antrim eyebrows'[1] all possessed sufficient attractions to make their parents expect that they would find husbands. But Mary and Jane

[1] Their mother, Lady Helen Macgregor was a daughter of the ninth Earl of Antrim. The Antrim eyebrow was the special feature legacy of Antrim beauty.

Findlater had restless, probing, growing minds and not nearly enough scope for them.

Already the pair were something of a terror and a menace to the young, often raw ministers who came to take duty for their father at Lochearnhead during the last years of his ministry, when his failing health made frequent help necessary. Mary and Jane would discuss, argue and dispute with the visiting preachers until the unfortunate young men were out of their depth and utterly bewildered. One of them, after prolonged controversy, defiantly thrust his flushed face round the parlour door as he went off to church, exclaiming after his ordeal, 'I don't care what ye say! I shall gie them a guid Gospel sairmon!'[1]

Mr. Findlater never really recovered his health and strength. His life had been far from easy and during the first years of the Disruption, he endured hardships of which he said little and complained less, but which, it was thought, gradually took their toll. Despite the doctor's assurances to the contrary, he knew, with Highland prescience, when death was near. Quietly, he discussed with his wife plans for her future. Then, one evening, appearing better after a short relapse, he sat in an arm-chair beside her and put his hand in hers. 'I gave it to her long years ago, Agnes,' he said to the maid, who had come into the room, 'to her sorrow and mine!' With a smile and a sigh and the echo of his affectionate little jest scarcely faded into silence, Eric Findlater died on 2nd May, 1886.

In his memory and to send to friends and parishioners, his wife and daughters had printed a small copy of his favourite and beloved Gospel of St. John. Some of the recipients objected to the small crosses finishing the corners of the little surround on the title-page. What would they have thought about the occasion when an Anglican clergyman preached for Mr. Findlater in his absence, and took a service in the little Presbyterian church?

Several years previously he and Mrs. Findlater had decided that they could no longer believe in Everlasting Punishment and it is easy to understand how alien such an idea would have been to

[1] Miss Gertrude Gray told me this story.

one of his temperament, whose whole nature responded to the Gospel of the Apostle of Love.

Some of its message seemed traced upon his calm expression as he slept away his last breaths. Death enhanced the statuesque beauty of his limbs and features. Except for a silvering of the black hair the dark youth was easily recalled, strangely little changed as he lay there, from the lad who had been called 'The Black Prince' at Aberdeen, when he went up to the University, as he wrote in his diary, 'too young'!

The girls, to whom their father had seemed a remote person, now felt as if his death had removed the very corner-stone of their lives, or suddenly taken away the protecting walls of the house.

Life at Lochearnhead had indeed come to an end for them. They were to return, often enough on visits there or to the neighbourhood, especially to Ardvorlich, but the manse, where they had grown up from babyhood, would be their home no more.

2

Prestonpans, First Novels

It was well for the three girls, now in or approaching their twenties, to quit a spot in those days so remote as Lochearnhead. There were many arrangements to be made between the May of 1886 and the following Christmas. The library and the coffee-house were left in the charge of Charlotte Stewart and everything was done to make possible the continuance of Mrs. Findlater's good works in various directions.

Mary and Jane deeply felt the uprooting. Mora was thankful to leave a place which she had felt to be mentally and physically stifling. Even Mary described their environment as 'like the bottom of a tea-cup' and declared that never normally had they seen the sun rise or set. This was a revelation of beauty which they were to experience when they went to Prestonpans and saw its evening glory over Edinburgh and the first light showing along the low coastline. After the enclosing mountains of Lochearnhead, that new landscape seemed strangely open and exposed.

. . . low hills, like waves stilled and grass-grown, few trees, nothing to attract the fancy except the quick rolling and changing of the cloud shadows, and the faint purples and greens of the inconspicuous undulations – and the great road running on and on – fair, open and suggestive as far as the eye could see.[1]

The advice and recommendations of the Borthwick Aunts took the Findlaters to this locality. In the autumn of 1886, the mother, her three daughters and one maid moved into Harlawhill,[2] a

[1] Mary Findlater, *The Rose of Joy*, London, 1903, p. 9.

[2] V. Nigel Tranter, *The Fortalices and Early Mansions of Southern Scotland*, 1400 to 1650, pubd. 1935, p. 59.

picturesque, seventeenth-century house at the east end of Prestonpans village.

Mary used to say that before this time, although during her
father's life they were poor enough, they had never noticed it
greatly. Now, Mrs. Findlater and her three daughters had to live
on a tiny income and they felt the pinch. Jane had insisted that
they must go near a coal mine to make ends meet, and at Prestonpans they got a cart-load for four and six. Fish also was cheap and
fresh. They were obliged to patronize the village dressmaker for
their clothes, and the girls became extremely conscious of the
quaint cut and the cheap materials, which seemed to advertise
poverty and lack of taste. For shoes they went into Edinburgh,
where at a shop 'on one of the bridges' they bought 'paper shoes'
for one and eight a pair.

Harlawhill was better to look at than to live in. It was large,
draughty and faced north, situated at a road fork, one prong of
which was the main route to Edinburgh. The beautiful, vast
Adams drawing-room on the first floor, with its white paint and
great blue shields designed upon the walls, and green damask
curtains, seemed to concentrate the cold. It was like an ice-house,
and the dining-room below it was scarcely better. Eventually
the shivering inmates moved their dining-room to the back which
looked out upon a sometimes sunny, walled garden, where in the
brief summer the ladies occasionally took tea on a bright afternoon. But for nearly three-quarters of the year the fierce winds
attacked the none too warmly clad persons of the sisters. Clothes,
especially thick coats, were expensive. Mary and Jane often remarked in later years upon the stupidity, with their income, of
attempting to keep servants. Wages were small enough in those
days, but they were a serious drain on slender means. Housework,
as they were to discover, could be a resource, giving them em-
ployment for at least a part of the days which so often exasperated
Mary and Jane by their apparent emptiness and futility.

The Findlaters were not lonely or isolated at Prestonpans and
they were welcomed by the small society there, which consisted
mainly of three families, Sprotts, Hislops and Lukes. There were

little parties at each other's houses, there was a chess club, and what Mary described as an 'attempt at an Essay Club'.

Soon they were to meet the Cadells of Cockenzie House. Mary and Jane made a friendship for life with the Colonel and most especially among his children with Annie and Marion. These two were younger than the Findlater sisters, but they found them interesting and unusual, particularly noting Marion as a remarkable young person. She, with her practical imagination and inventiveness, with her wonderful vitality which she seemed able to communicate to other creatures, human or animal, as a lifesaving force, had much to give Mary and Jane. Ever undaunted by her own troubles, which were often overwhelming enough, she was ready to travel from one end of the land to the other at a few moments' notice if her two friends needed help or comfort. How often Mary and Jane used to say, 'There are states of mind when *only* the company of Marion Cadell can stiffen us up.'[1]

Friends and acquaintances at Prestonpans were certainly far from colourless, and some of them might well have been placed there by a considerate Providence as 'good copy' for a pair of future novelists.

There was the elderly Miss Cunningham, sister of the lady who, at the age of sixty, as Mary used to put it, 'undertook marriage with old Sir Robert Cadell'.[2] This was not her only claim to interest, for when she first came to call on Mrs. Findlater at Harlawhill, Mary's fascinated gaze became riveted on a curious excrescence at the back of the lady's head. The object appeared to be a handsome ball of wool. 'Yes', remarked Miss Cunningham, answering the young woman's thoughts, 'it was just a ball of grey wool I saw lying on my toilet table. It matched my hair so perfectly that I simply fastened it on.'

Another local character was Miss Sprott of Northfield.[3] She

[1] Mary Findlater, letter to Marion Cadell, 22nd February, 1928.

[2] Uncle of the Findlaters' friends, Annie and Marion Cadell.

[3] Miss Sprott rented Northfield House from the McNeills. Mr. James McNeill, a mining engineer from Renfrewshire had bought it in 1896, and it remained in his family until 1951. It is a fine Jacobean mansion, and a rare survival from times and circumstances in Scotland usually too primitive,

had settled down in this beautiful old house with a family of nieces and their mother. The widowed Mrs. Sprott had once confided to Mary and Jane that hers was largely a life of self-abnegation. Miss Sprott had, in fact, made it a condition that she should be mistress not only in what was, of course, her own house, but that she should also have complete control over the upbringing of the girls. Mrs. Sprott was in no position to refuse the offer.

Despite her somewhat exacting conditions, Miss Sprott desired her intentions to be Christian and charitable. She often prefaced a remark with 'Not wishing to say anything in the least disagreeable...' This formula had particularly delighted Mary and Jane when it was followed by the comment, 'I find Mr.— a *very* repulsive young man!' Mr.— was a would-be and not very acceptable suitor for one of the nieces. The matrimonial affairs of her adopted family weighed heavily upon Miss Sprott, until she had all the girls married. On the whole the matches were to her satisfaction and doubtless her task was one of steering rather than manufacturing, as the nieces were attractive young women with rose petal complexions.

The high, white-harled walls of Northfield would have provided a setting for a fairy-tale princess, even to the little turrets and upper windows that for the passer-by below invited a glimpse of some lovely face or a glint of bright hair. There was pleasant seclusion too for the young people and their swains in the large high-walled garden on summer days, but harsh weather often made the house a necessary refuge. There in the drawing-room, Miss Sprott presided and persistently remained to chaperon the engaged couples, according to the conventions of the time, or rather of those nearer her own girlhood. She would seat herself at her writing-table and with flagrant tact become preoccupied with her correspondence. At intervals, however, to the good-

---

politically disturbed and war-ridden for purely domestic architecture. V. Nigel Tranter, *The Fortalices and Early Mansions of Southern Scotland*, 1400 to 1650, 1935, pp. 62–63.

Inventory of Monuments and Constructions in the County of East Lothian pubd. by The Royal Commission on Ancient and Historical Monuments and Constructions of Scotland, 1924, pp. 104–57, and an article by Sheila Forman *in Scotlands Magazine*, May 1961, pp. 23–26 natured amusement of the nieces, she would lift her head, exclaiming brightly for the encouragement of those concerned, 'I see nothing, I hear nothing.'

Stimulated, maybe, by the example of previous occupants,[1] whose piety had found an expression more permanent and modestly decorative, Miss Sprott had sprinkled texts in profusion all over the house, selecting for the bathroom one which fascinated the imagination of the Findlater sisters. 'The Jew first and then the Gentile.'

Throughout the first year at Prestonpans they both did a good deal of desultory writing, but little came of it. In the early nineties they were seeing much of their mother's kinswoman, Mary Maclagan, and meeting her friends. Some of these were people of a type they had scarcely encountered before, and they felt their knowledge of the world, of human nature and of culture was both enlarged and enriched. Here was life and excitement. Prestonpans, by contrast, seemed dull and flat when they returned to it.

There were, however, excitements, less welcome now and then. One summer night, when the Harlawhill household was in bed and asleep except for Mary who was, characteristically, wakeful, there were sounds which disturbed her, coming apparently from the garden below. She roused Jane, who sleepily complained that her sister was 'always imagining things'. Mary was sure that she heard voices, got up and looked out of the window. There was moonlight enough to reveal two men trying to get in at the kitchen window, and Jane used to declare that in announcing this fact Mary's subdued tones had in them an indubitable ring of triumph and satisfaction.

That night, so it happened, there were no servants in the building. Mora was away, and their mother with their two selves comprised the somewhat defenceless household. As Mary rapidly reviewed this vulnerable and unpleasant situation, she looked

[1] In a moulded architrave about the entrance doorway in the centre of the South wall is inscribed 'Excep. the. Lord. buld. inwae. bulds. man.' There was also (it is now concealed) a monitory verse above the heads of the laird and his lady in the bedroom added by Joseph Marjoribanks in 1611.

round desperately for a weapon. Her eye fell on the fireplace. Quickly she seized the old iron fender, dragged it to the open window, somehow levered it on to the sill, and with the strength of desperation pushed it over, so that it fell with a bomblike crash on the paved path below.

Startled and terrified beyond measure, the would-be burglars fled precipitately. One of them entangled himself in the clothes line on the drying field, before finally getting off with his companion. Mary next roused their nearest neighbour, and he went to fetch the police, but all this took so much time (for her knocks were not heard at first, and the neighbour's dressing operations caused further delay) that the thieves got away and were never caught. For this the girls were scarcely sorry, and Mary's relief was immense in realizing that she had not killed anyone. Looking back on the incident, she was less concerned at any complications for herself that might have ensued than with the misery she would have felt at 'killing anyone . . . I should have been so *dreadfully* depressed' she used to say, with an emphatic rolling of the continental R which was a characteristic of her speech.

Summer passed pleasantly enough as a rule, with these visits to friends in various parts of the country, and at home the lighter skies, with a measure of warmth for a few all too brief months. Even in August, which can produce the heaviest weather in Scotland, the air was invigorating at Prestonpans.

In 1893 Mary and Jane made their first expedition to London. This was on the whole a cheerful and diverting experience. Mary records their first walk in Kensington Gardens on Sunday, 19th February, 1893. They stayed with Charlotte Stewart and her mother 'at Stamford Row'[1] from where they 'paid visits' and 'saw London', often conducted by Charlotte's friend 'young Mr. Hopkinson'. At the end of March they went to Polesworth[2] to stay into April with old friends of their mother's, the Potters. Of this Mary writes:

It was lovely weather. We saw the English spring for the first

[1] Chelsea.   [2] Warwickshire.

time. A green tree against the blue sky one day when we went up the river, was a revelation.[1]

Until 1895, the order of events throughout the year settled down upon certain lines. The summer was more or less enjoyable, but winters were wretchedly cold and depressing, with hardships aggravated by illness and incursions of Borthwick aunts. Jane persisted through all difficulties in her attempts to write, earning a little money by a short story here and there[2] and throughout the harsh winter of 1894, often ill and always anxious about ways and means, she was engaged on a novel built from the story, often told by their mother in times past, about her girlhood's friend and correspondent, Georgina Moncrieff. This winter was 'fearfully cold' and during some of the worst weather the sisters stayed with Mrs. Macgillivray at Lairg Lodge, where Mary 'read aloud Jane's MS to her' and underlines in her diary 'she fell asleep as I read'.[3]

Poverty which winced and shivered at the fierce thrust of a Scottish winter in those exposed regions of the country, Mary and Jane knew full well. Not only was it impossible for them to buy clothes sufficiently good and warm to defend their bodies from the piercing winds; they could not even afford the materials needed for the manuscript of a book. Jane managed to get for her *Green Graves* discarded sheets of paper, about foolscap size, from the local grocer. Upon some of them, the pencilled names of customers are still visible, on pages subsequently filled by graceful, clear handwriting. Jane must have exercised perfect control over the scratchy nib and broken little penholder, which was the only tool she had to produce pages which might be the envy of handwriting experts. The manuscript embodies in large measure, the precious life-blood of spoken narrative art, for the story is written unhesitatingly, with scarcely an erasure, just as the fluent teller would have told it, to beguile long winter evenings.

[1] Summary Diary for 1893.

[2] *Allan Grey: An Indigent Gentlewoman,* published in No. 38. *The Pseudonym Library* together with *The Hon. Stanbury* and *Miss Skeet,* two short stories by Charlotte Stewart.

[3] Summary Diary.

In 1895 both the sisters felt more cheerful because they were occupied. Mary was writing a book which was to be published later as *A Narrow Way*, she was getting together a small collection of her poems and attending 'Mr. Macgregor's studio in Edinburgh.'[1] Her gift for painting was considerable and at this time her allegiance was divided between art and literature.

The real event of 1895, however, took place when an unpretentious little letter written in script came to Jane from Methuen saying that her *Green Graves* contained work of excellent quality 'and they would be happy to publish it'.

This book marked the turning point of the sisters' fortunes, worldly and otherwise. What ever trials and anxieties Mary and Jane had to face in the future, and there were plenty, their lives were now to be lived on a different level. Obscurity and poverty no longer hemmed them in or oppressed them unduly. The way to fame was open. They were accepted by the intelligentsia of the day, of whatever rank in society.

All this did not come to them with one dramatic gesture of Fate. It was a change which manifested itself over the course of two or three years, but it was swift enough.

At the end of February 1896, the first copies of the *Green Graves* arrived. In March Mary became ill and Aunt Jane installed herself at Harlawhill, adding 'much to our fatigues', though it is only fair to record that Aunt Jane added sometimes to her nieces' amusement. She would, for instance, retire to the sofa or arm-chair in her bedroom to escape for a short while from what she called 'the turmoil', drape her black silk handkerchief over her head (it was specially kept for the purpose) and fall asleep. This was no doubt a sensible and salubrious plan, but Mary and Jane could not help wondering what 'turmoil' could make a ripple enough to oscillate the tiniest fly upon the smooth surface of the little backwater in which Aunt Jane's life was now secluded. Even more did they smile, when the old lady, oblivious of changed modes and customs, pointed out that it would be suitable for Mora (then in her thirties) to 'wear a little something up here'. Admonishing Mary

[1] Summary Diary.

and Jane to give their sister a hint of this, she indicated the exact position for a lace cap with a few significant light taps on the top of her own head, conjuring up for their imaginations a decidedly ludicrous vision.

In the spring of 1896 when Mary returned from a visit to Matlock with Miss Sprott and one of her nieces, what she had scarcely been aware of before was brought into relief by that interval. Jane met her in Edinburgh.

'I realized (Mary wrote) that the success of her book was changing her.' She looked much better and happier than ever before. In truth throughout the years 1896–7, the gates of the literary and intellectual worlds were opening for the sisters. The names of these two women now possessed significance. It was clear from the reception of Jane's book that any work of hers or of Mary's would be regarded with interest.

Colonel Cadell brought Richard Haldane, then Liberal Member for Haddington, to tea at Harlawhill, and Mr. Haldane declared that he hardly liked to sit down in the presence of so distinguished a person as the authoress of *The Green Graves*. However 'dated' such an attitude to a woman writer might be, the remark, coming from this man, certainly adds to the general sense of importance in the impression that the book was making upon the public.

Lady Wemyss and Lady Frances Balfour were callers at this time and became frequent visitors. When in February 1897 Mary and Jane were in London, they were invited to Lady Frances Balfour's House of Commons parties, dining at least twice there.[1] Mary used to say that 'Jane looked so small between the Prime Minister[2] and the Chancellor of the Exchequer'[3] but her pride and joy in her sister was intense when her own eminent neighbour (a Minister whose name she did not remember) asked, 'Which of you is the distinguished authoress of *The Green Graves*?'

[1] Summary Diary, February 1897.

[2] The third Marquess of Salisbury.

[3] Sir Michael Hicks-Beach. Lady Frances's brother-in-law, Arthur Balfour, was First Lord of the Treasury.

Their pleasure in being fêted was checked even now, when they had a little money, by the feeling that they could not afford to dress sufficiently well for these occasions. When in after years Lady Frances, reminiscing, happened to say how charming they had looked at her parties in their pretty dresses which were so 'exactly right', the sisters could not help exclaiming: 'Oh, Lady Frances, if only you could have told us so then, we should have been infinitely reassured.'

The Westminster Gazette of 11th July, 1896, recorded under the heading Literary Notes and News:

Mr. Gladstone has been reading a great deal lately in the intervals between his theological studies, which occupy the best part of every day. One of the stories which charmed him most is The Green Graves of Balgowrie by Jane Findlater, a new writer.

In the autumn of this year (1896) Miss Constance Gladstone wrote to a friend:[1]

We were much interested to hear something more about the authoress of the Green Graves etc. and I hope some day you will tell me more – My uncle Mr. Gladstone was much struck with it indeed.

Please send to the authoress for me. I meant to write. . . . She may like the G.O.M.'s compliment.

Yours very sincerely,

Constance E. Gladstone.

The following summer, after their Aunt Jane Borthwick's death in August, the Findlaters decided to spend the winter in Cornwall, largely for their mother's health, and in September they settled to take the Rectory at Marham Church, North Cornwall. It was while they were there that Jane received an enthusiastic letter from Ellen Terry, forwarded by Methuen. The great actress wrote on 9th January, 1898, from 22 Barkston Gardens, Earls Court, S.W.

[1] A pencil note from which the beginning has disappeared.

Dear Jane Helen Findlater,

I had a delightful first day of this year, for I 'helped' in the production of a young friend's play, and read *right through*, at a sitting, *The Green Graves of Balgowrie* – & whilst I was *acting* in the *Play* I thought upon the *book*. Delightful – Delightful – I love it – & thank you for it. I must snatch a pause in my life fritterings very soon, & read it again —

May I ask why, on the title page, no mention is made of *other* work of yours —? I long to read more of you.

I can only send you my gratitude, & wish towards you most affectionately —

Truly Yours,
Ellen Terry.

Next autumn they met in Edinburgh. Ellen Terry wrote to Jane from The Royal Hotel (Macgregor's) on 5th October, 1898:

I am never 'disengaged' but pray *engage* me on Friday. I have to go to an Actors' Fund meeting at 12. *I wish you wd go with me.'* and then after a short drive, return with me to this Hotel to luncheon. ['At 3.30 I must go into a dark room & rest' is firmly crossed out and the letter continues]

Will you, *will you* chime in with these arrangements. It would give me so much pleasure — I can't say how delighted I was to get your letter this morning. Thank you – *for all* — The dear *Green Graves* stand out in my memory still as one of the best books in the world —

Yours very sincerely,
Ellen Terry.

Thus, and with such distinguished names together with innumerable humbler ones, did Jane's 'fan mail', as it would now be called, grow, and reviews were laudatory.

At Marham Church in Cornwall the Findlaters remained until June 1898. A delightful Christmas picnic at Widemouth was a new experience to people nurtured on Scottish winters. But the coming eighteen months were to be among the darkest in their lives, for Mora became mentally ill. For Jane, Mary and their mother poverty, anxiety and poor health aggravated and intensified one another.

Their friends rallied round. The Borthwick aunts, hitherto oblivious of the need close at hand, shouldered the financial burden. Ever turning towards enlightened knowledge, as flowers to the sun, Mary and Jane found solace and support in learning from Sir John Batty Tuke, the great brain specialist, who attended their sister, of the new attitude towards and treatment of mental disorders. They steadfastly continued their novel writing. A little money was coming in from their books. They had the unaccustomed thrill of buying for their mother an exquisitely made warm white shawl and for themselves 'coats at Maules'. They were invited to meet the Rudyard Kiplings at Dunrobin. During sojourns in Edinburgh, William Macgregor[1] had become a frequent visitor at Ann Street when they were there.

Through the sombre warp of their fortunes brighter threads were beginning to show. It was Mora, at home again, and almost fully recovered by the summer of 1900, who persuaded her mother and sisters to go with her to Embleton, with consequences delightful and enriching for Mary and Jane.

They were invited to Fallodon for the first time on 23rd August. Mary and Jane had hesitated about accepting this invitation but they went, albeit without any particular pleasure at the prospect. A previous meeting with Lady Grey, when she had come to call on them, had left no very favourable impression. Her manner had appeared abrupt and cold. Even her best friends used to feel this about her in general company, and the barrier of shyness (for such it was) repelled the casual acquaintance. But the sisters very speedily changed their opinion when they went to spend the afternoon with her at Fallodon. After one half-hour of her company, so Jane declared, the first feelings had been supplanted by those of a very different kind. A new planet, as Mary put it, had

[1] The Very Reverend William Malcolm Macgregor D.D., L.L.D., b. 1861, d. 1944. Moderator of the Free Church of Scotland 1919, held distinguished lectureships and wrote books on various religious subjects. Became Professor of N.T. Exegesis at Trinity College, Glasgow, 1919–35, and was Principal 1928–38.

swum into their ken, one that altered the look of the dark sky. Here was a woman, they felt, quite unlike anyone else they had ever met, and a most vividly interesting personality. This impression both sisters carried to the end, and far from fading, it deepened as the years went by.

Later, on 10th September, Mary and Jane went with Lady Grey on an expedition to Holy Island, and from that time they were much at Fallodon during their visit, meeting there Mrs. Creighton[1] and Mrs. Phillimore. Meanwhile they had been obliged to move into lodgings yet more uncomfortable and Mrs. Findlater had become ill again. By 24th September Mary had fallen a victim to influenza and Jane was being worn out with looking after the invalids. Lady Grey, hearing of these misfortunes, descended like a *deus ex machina* on to the troubled stage. But more beautiful and warm-hearted than any stage goddess, she would have carried off the whole family to convalesce at Fallodon had this been possible. Her imperial kindness would have speedily brought this about had she not always been open to reason and argument, with an ardent desire to get at the truth, whether abstract or practical. Finally, when she understood all the circumstances, it was decided between her and Jane that Mary should be taken to Fallodon and Mrs. Findlater, who was scarcely able for any move, left at the lodgings in Jane's care.

Thus Mary was carried off, under some protest, to be nursed at Fallodon, and while she recovered there, Lady Grey sent down to Mrs. Findlater and her devoted nurse every material comfort available. Yet as Jane declared, and Mary was now beginning to learn more fully, this sort of kindness was the least valuable thing that Lady Grey had to offer, for with her gift she gave herself, in a way possible to few people and not many had comparable treasure to bestow.

The steel-true sincerity which ran through every fibre of her being was perhaps Lady Grey's most impressive quality. Mary used to say that her keen, piercing questions were like rapier

[1] Wife of the Bishop of London, Rt. Hon. Rev. Mandell Creighton, 1897–1901.

thrusts. But the blade was tempered by great zest for life and intense sympathy for all things living. She had a heart for everything that was noble. Although no one could be more outspoken or down-to-earth, she seemed to raise the whole level of life above the commonplace or the ordinary. She demanded and received the very best from her friends. Mary and Jane felt her influence working as a wonderful antidote and cure after the nerve strain and anxiety of their sister's illness.

Lady Grey's appearance matched her character, for she possessed uncommon beauty of person, a commanding presence, a natural, stately grace. Her charming voice enhanced every sentence she uttered, but over and above this she could endow a hackneyed word or phrase with new life and more intense meaning. Used by her, the overdone and exhausted word 'nice', for example, seemed to take on something of its medieval freshness and significance. A simple remark or judgement on her lips acquired unforgettable significance, as when she exclaimed to Mary, during a discussion on marriage and home life, 'Families were meant to separate' and on another occasion, 'There are no classes, only individuals.'

With all these fine and serious qualities, there mingled a delicious sense of humour and fun, an almost tempestuous energy, promptitude and competence in action, when it had to be taken, and yet the ability to give a sense of calm and repose to her friends even when she herself was disturbed and anxious. It was not for nothing that Dorothy Grey had been born a Widdrington, and was thus linked with a heroic episode in one of the fine Border Ballads, Chevy Chase. Simplicity, beauty, decision of movement characterized her physically.

Her marriage to Sir Edward was one of those perfect matches where each partner enriches the other's best. They both loved the country, country pursuits and a retired life, but entered the political arena with a sense of dedication and the will to give to the utmost. They have been accused of too great a desire to live in an Arcadia, however high-souled, of their own making, and of lacking any sense of reality about 'those things' which were 'coming on the earth'. But this supposed want of prevision, shared with many of the eminent persons of that time, is a shortcoming difficult to assess in definite terms, and who shall judge of the necessity to high endeavour and heavy public responsibility, of those periods of retired pleasure in rural surroundings at Itchen or Fallodon, which they loved so well? Sir Edward might have escaped some of the censure which has fallen upon him had he not tried to share their charm by writing of them, and especially of birds, in such a beguiling fashion.

Be this as it may, their homes and privileges were shared with others, the cottage at Itchen lent to special friends, and those in trouble, mental or physical, were succoured and cherished at Fallodon. A large, friendly red-brick house, it stood on sloping ground a few miles from sea and moor, surrounded, though not overshadowed, by great old trees, with gardens inclining down to a small stretch of water. Mary described it as 'not specially beautiful' but having a character and dignity of its own. Its peace, order and spaciousness, after the cramped conditions of uncomfortable lodgings, were a great restorative. Especially did the convalescent enjoy the evenings there, when after the day's rest she would dress and come down to join Sir Edward and Lady Grey in the Library. They were always involved in some book, which he would read aloud, and there, tucked up on the sofa, supported by its white silk cushions, Mary lay and listened to a George Meredith novel made the more vivid by Sir Edward's keen enjoyment and hearty laughter, or Dorothy Grey's comments, as she sat near her guest, with hands usually employed in some needlework (Sir Edward rather disapproved of knitting, maintaining that it was an excuse for mental idleness) and the time slipped by with golden and benign influence in its wake.

It was not until a year or so later that alterations were made at Fallodon, converting five rooms into two, and Lady Grey had a new drawing-room which she liked so much that she inhabited it more than the old library. The home that Mary and Jane Findlater first knew was the old one to which Sir Edward had brought his bride in 1885, when the library was still their special sanctum.

It looked out through large windows to the great beeches on the lawn and its walls were lined with books whose bindings were faded and mellowed by age and sunshine. It was a warm and quiet room, as Mary recalled it, full of the sweet scents of flowers grouped in pots and vases which covered the whole of one table. Modern books had been added to the older classics and there were two efficient looking writing-tables. Truly it was a pleasant place to work in, to muse in, or in which to find health for body, mind and spirit.

By early October the cure had worked, and Mary was able to return to Embleton. She was taken back triumphantly in the new car, one of the first known in that neighbourhood, if not quite the first. Before they set out her hostess reassured her, 'The journey will be perfectly safe,' she said, 'for Edward will walk or run beside us.' 'Which he did,' added Mary, 'all the way.'

The other invalid, Mrs. Findlater, had not made such a complete recovery. The doctor prescribed a milder climate for the winter, a climate where there would be a less severe drop in the temperature at night, as the only hope for survival. The sisters, therefore, after various inquiries, took a house for the winter at Beer in Devonshire, and the family set off in October, by rail, travelling all night in an invalid carriage. Mrs. Findlater's difficult breathing seemed eased, even in the train, as soon as it passed into the region of milder, south-western air. The party arrived on the following day at Seaton in Devon, and in the early afternoon drove to Beer, where they installed themselves in a shabby little villa, kept by an old Mrs. Whiston. There they became acquainted with their neighbours, the Astors and Trevelyans, and there Mary wrote *Betty Musgrave* and Jane produced the poorest of her novels, *The Story of a Mother*.

Mrs. Findlater could no longer winter in Scotland and so it came about that the family was transplanted in the following year to Devon. At first the change seemed not too alien to Mary and Jane. They found a house, 'Southfield Mount', at Paignton, a house which charmed them with its little courtyard, its minute garden raised like a balcony and the view of orchards and sea from the windows. Mora was now devotedly working as a nurse at East Ham, having at last found her vocation. The Paignton neighbours, among whom was Jack Yeats the painter, brother of W. B. Yeats, were congenial spirits. Old friends came to stay at Southfield or near by. Mary was writing *The Rose of Joy* and they were happy. But the lease of Southfield ran out all too soon and wearied with fruitless searching they took Mount Stuart at Torquay and moved there from Paignton in May 1902.

They disliked it at first sight and this was a bad beginning, for to Mary and Jane, houses were almost personalities, which by their character could affect the whole tenor of life. They disliked also the red cliffs and heavy, luxuriant vegetation of Torquay. The lush growth represented something wholly alien to their natures, so utterly different was it from the clear cut, stark beauty of the north. The soft climate which helped their mother was enervating and exhausting to them. Mary was assailed by depression, not quite so deep perhaps as that which attacked the Rudyard Kiplings in the spring of '96 when they rented a house in Mary Church but the mood induced was dreary and discouraging enough.

The Findlaters now began to make their first acquaintance with Torquay and Torquay people. The period of the great hostesses there was waning. The reign of the Duchess of Sutherland[1] from Sutherland Tower, Torquay, had ended more than a decade earlier. Money not mind was beginning to rule and persist in this growing seaside resort. Through the streets and drives and the new roads, which were piercing through the former quiet pasture and woodland, bowled carriages taking wealthy invalids and pampered well-to-do women for their daily outings.

But always the great point in favour of Devon and its climate was that Mrs. Findlater became better and stronger there, and neither of her authoress daughters was impervious to the charm of the real countryside or more remote villages, lying as it were concealed even in broad sunshine among low growing gnarled trees through which the light pierced only here and there in a

[1] Anne Hay–Mackenzie, who became the wife of the 3rd Duke of Sutherland in 1849. She was Mistress of the Robes, 1870–74.

golden spear. The little houses, low and often garlanded with blossom looked to the sisters like the dwellings of elves rather than human beings. There were fascinating glimpses of doors within doors, and little courtyards. The head of an old woman with wrinkled face and white cap appearing at a casement window, a couple of little children tottering down low stone steps, hand in hand, a patch of brilliant grass, buttercups, a black cat sitting in sunlight by an open door – suggested to these ladies from the north a world of fairy-tale.

Dartmoor, however, appeared to them travesty of a Scottish moor, and when Mary and Jane went for a week with their friends Kate Riggs (better known as Kate Douglas Wiggin)[1] and Charlotte Stewart to Hay Tor, the mists and rains descended. The party was house-bound. 'Now girls', exclaimed the irrepressible Kate as she came downstairs on the second dismal, streaming wet morning, 'we can't go out . . . We must collaborate over a book.'[2] It was to be a lightsome affair. Each lady chose a different character to impersonate. Mary took the fussy rigid old lady, Kate Riggs the gay American heroine, Charlotte Stewart the hero and Jane a contrasting and slightly down-trodden English girl.

The Findlaters were now becoming acquainted with Torquay people far more congenial than those first encountered. Their new friends included Miss Vulliamy, George Meredith's sister-in-law. From her they learnt many things of Meredith's life and character and how impossible it was for any woman to live with this greatly gifted writer (much admired by the Findlaters and by Miss Vulliamy herself) for, said his sister-in-law, he was a ceaseless nagger. If, for instance, his wife came down to breakfast, wearing a collar he did not like, he would start the day with criticisms, continue the theme at lunch-time, and as the evening shades prevailed, return to it again. That such a champion of women in their struggles

[1] Kate Douglas Wiggin who afterwards became Mrs. Riggs was an American authoress. She was born in 1856 and died in 1923. Her maiden name was Smith. She wrote numerous books, many of which were for children and young people. She was probably best known for her *Rebecca of Sunnybrook Farm*, London, 1903.

[2] *The Affair at the Inn,* 1904

for freedom and equality with man, such a masterly depicter of delightful feminine characters should be able to make the life of one woman so unbearable, is one of the freaks of irony.

Existence in Torquay was not wholly monotonous. It could provide adventure of a kind. On a mild day in 1902 when the sisters were peacefully sitting on a bench near the edge of a cliff in what was then known as Manor Gardens, they noticed coming round the bend towards them in this secluded spot, a strange-looking man. As he approached they saw, to their horror that he was foaming at the mouth. Before they could utter a word or a cry, this terrifying creature was upon them. He attacked Mary, knocked off her hat and seizing her by the hair began to drag her towards the cliff edge. Jane had become almost petrified with horror and the situation was only saved by the appearance of a large dog round the corner. The assailant was startled, and as a man and woman came upon the scene close behind the dog, the lunatic, for such he was, let go his victim, and rushed away, making his escape as best he could. The owner of the dog hastened to give the alarm and the maniac was captured shortly afterwards attempting some other criminal act.

Mary and Jane welcomed an escape now and then from Torquay to see their friends in London and it was during one of these visits that Jane had a luncheon engagement with Lady Grey. Her hostess had just arrived from Scotland where she had been lunching on the previous day with Lord Rosebery at Dalmeny. The Duchess of Sutherland was of the party.[1] Both she and Lord Rosebery, with several others, tried to persuade Lady Grey to postpone her return to London. Lady Grey, however, pleaded engagements on the following afternoon and mentioned that she was 'expecting Miss Findlater to lunch'.

'Findlater!' echoed the Duchess. 'But of course – I know all about the Findlaters. Their father was not the son of the old minister at Durness, but the child of a Spanish pirate whose ship was storm stayed there. The Minister's wife used to visit him on board ship . . . Everyone in Durness knew.'

[1] Millicent, Duchess of Sutherland.

It was characteristic of the forthright Lady Grey that almost immediately on meeting Jane, she exclaimed, 'You never told me about your Spanish grandfather!' Jane looked at her hostess in blank amazement, then listened incredulously to the tale that followed.

Next day, back at Torquay, she told it with a laugh at the family luncheon table, exclaiming at the wild and extraordinary tales that some people could fabricate and others believe. But the sisters' amusement was suddenly checked when they saw that their mother, far from laughing with them, looked very grave. Presently she said quietly, 'Well, my dears, since you have heard the story in this way, I will tell you.'

She then disclosed how a relative, Colonel Horsborough[1], had ridden post-haste from the far north and arrived on the eve of her wedding at her father's house in Claremont Crescent. He demanded to see Mr. Borthwick and with great agitation told him the strange tale of Eric Findlater's parentage, the authenticity of which he did not doubt. 'You cannot', he declared to Mr. Borthwick, 'you cannot allow your daughter to marry this man.'

Mary and Jane were impressed and even amazed that this gentle little Victorian mother, whose young womanhood had been so carefully fenced about within high walls of Victorian proprieties and restrictions, had then taken command.

'Mr. Findlater,' she said calmly and decidedly, 'is the man I love. It does not matter to me who his father was. All I ask is that nothing more shall be said about this, ever. It is clear that Eric knows nothing of it, or he would have told me.' Of this she remained convinced, and nothing was ever said, nor did the knowledge ever cast the slightest shadow over her married happiness.

What afterwards became for the two writers a rather fascinating but unfathomable human story, was at first something of a shock. They rose from the table feeling as if the four walls of their house had suddenly been removed. Respectability had been torn from them just at the point where it seemed absolutely secure. As soon as possible, Mary, who would never have been content to leave

[1] One of the Horsboroughs of Maloney.

such a problem unravelled, went out to see their old friend Mrs. Gordon, who was then a neighbour, hoping and expecting to receive from her an incontrovertible reputation of the strange legend.

Mrs. Gordon was a sweet, gentle, greatly admired and loved old lady, possessed of singular charm, wisdom and perfection of character and no friend to scandal. She had lived for much of her youth in Durness, and 'knew everybody'. She smiled as her young friend broke the painful news, but instead of the looked for denial, to Mary's astonishment the reply was, 'But my dear, *everybody* in Durness *knew*!'

So everyone at Durness knew, and perhaps at Lochearnhead and elsewhere as well! It seemed that only those most concerned had been kept in ignorance. How could her father have failed to know? Mary and Jane did not share their mother's absolute conviction about this. It might explain his swarthy appearance, and their own dark complexions, but there was much about the story that did not satisfy their credulity.

Later in life, when Mary and Jane were examining some Reay portraits, they were suddenly struck by an unexpected and curious resemblance to themselves. Simultaneously and with one thought they looked at one another. They had been told that Eric, seventh Lord Reay,[1] had been one of their grandmother's special friends and admirers, and of how he had called at the manse on the very day of their father's birth. Inquiring what the child's names were to be, he was answered with hesitation and uncertainty by the servant who came to the door, 'Let him be called after me!' exclaimed his Lordship, and turned away.

So the child became Lord Reay's name son. He was called Eric John, and his daughters remembered how the desk he had always worked at had once belonged to Lord Reay. Could the Spanish pirate legend have served merely to cover up the true story? Had it, indeed, been put about for this purpose?

Practical problems and household worries precluded pursuit of this intriguing problem. Their Aunt Margaret Borthwick, a

[1] The Lords Reay were chiefs of the Clan Mackay, and resided for many generations in Sutherland.

typical Victorian invalid, her maid and a nurse were now installed at Mount Stuart and distracting battles raged between the Borthwick and Findlater retainers. Nevertheless, throughout all the trials and tribulations, the authoresses persistently clung to the quiet time which they had accustomed themselves to spend alone together each evening between tea and supper. It was then that they wrote, or if they did not put pen to paper, sat thinking over the next or the current novel.

3

American Tour

In the Autumn of 1904 a visit to America was being definitely planned. There had been talk of it with Kate Riggs and her sister, Nora Smith during the summer. The Findlaters' American publishers[1] had urged the desirability of such a visit and finally arranged it. The sisters were by this time authoresses of repute on either side of the Atlantic. Although self-advertisement was always repugnant to them, travel, a spice of adventure, the possibility of meeting new friends and new minds in a New World were irresistably attractive. In 1905 journeys of this kind were undertaken far less readily than today, especially by people of modest means. For the two ladies, who had previously not set foot beyond the island of Britain, an American tour was a considerable event. The outcome not only endorsed their previous literary success, it also put them on the road to the summit of their achievement.

Early in January the sisters left Torquay and travelled to Manchester where they stayed a couple of nights with their old friends, the Herbert Grays. On 11th January, escorted by Herbert, they came to Liverpool where he saw them on board the *Arabic*. They were now a party of three as Margaret Blaikie[2] had joined them at the port.

The voyage began in tempests and the travellers suffered accordingly during the first few days. Seas were calmer, however, towards the end of the journey, so that Mary and Jane were on their feet again, and able to enjoy the 'radiant winter morning' of their arrival. Mary's American Diary describes the visit.[3]

[1] Then McClure Phillips & Co.
[2] Daughter of Walter Blaikie, the publisher.
[3] Unless otherwise stated, all quotations in this chapter are from Mary's American Diary.

Mary and Jane were on deck as the *Arabic* steamed slowly up the river, and absorbed in the prospect before them, gazed at the tall buildings, red and white, reflecting in the water. Soon they were involved in the bustle of disembarking and were treated so cursorily at the customs house that Mary exclaimed to the official who had passed their baggage, that his work was a farce. He rounded on her, asking indignantly, 'Do you think I have no knowledge of human nature? One glance at your face showed me there was nothing in *your* boxes.'

Kate's husband, George Riggs met them and took them by carriage to 58th Street, swinging and jolting along the filthy uneven roads. At the end of their journey came Kate's delicious welcome. Upstairs as they unpacked there was a touch of strangeness in the big wooden bolsters covered in chintz laid on the bed during the day, and the pillows secreted in a chest.

The ebullient, warm-hearted and ever-active Kate gathered all her circle together to meet and admire her two friends. Much as Mary and Jane loved her they did not share all her tastes and likings. At Kate's afternoon reception on the first Saturday they found the richness of the women's dresses bewildering. Mary noted in her diary, 'fat woman with a diamond star pinned to her waist behind, the squeezing of hands, the eagerness to do the same thing, the good nature, smiling, restlessness.' The dresses at the Waldorf Astoria, the jewels as large as breakfast eggs at Tiffany's, touched the nerve of half-amused disgust in the sisters. They began to feel that size was the American criterion of beauty in ornament.

At Kate's dinner-parties they met few kindred spirits. When Miss Kitty Cheatham, an interpretative singer, who had written a pamphlet against the *Star Spangled Banner*, which she considered opposed to the true spirit of democracy, was a guest, Mary saw her as a Christian Scientist who was 'dressed in soiled white net', with 'a huge head of yellow hair.' Josephine Dodge Daskam Bacon, an authoress, seemed to have made little impression at all, perhaps because her husband dominated the conversation. He lived up to his formidable name of Selden Bacon by being in the legal profession, but endeavoured, not wholly successfully, to entertain the Findlaters with tales of ranch life.

New York had staged snow-storms soon after the sisters' arrival. When these had abated they sallied forth to buy boots, but the shop assistants were impatient and hustling, the boots bad and expensive. Returning from the theatre one night they felt the crush on the car most alarming. It seemed to be only the limpet force of the more solid strap-hangers which prevented the whole load being decanted by jolts and abrupt stops into a seething pile on the roadside. A combination of this tenacity, with perfectly good humour, alone saved the situation.

The days passed in concerts at the Waldorf, luncheon in the Palm Room, teas at Sherry's and dinner-parties in private apartments at the homes of Kate Riggs' friends. Now there were likes at first sight as well as dislikes. Seated on the broad sofa before a bright fire in a book lined room at the Ivans, Mary and Jane felt at home. Their hostess impressed them with her quiet integrity, their host and children with their interesting individuality. At the Smalley's there were fresh tea, comfortable chairs and an air of home and freedom at the same time. Kindness touched them when a fellow guest at a luncheon-party offered the services of her Japanese maid to repair the Findlaters' wardrobe, since they had confessed to having been unable to sew on a button or a braid in the rush of life since their arrival. They were immediately attracted to Margaret Deland,[1] 'bright, honest, delightful' in her little grey toque and pale-grey dress.

There were also emphatic dislikes, immediate and usually unalterable. At the Underwood Johnsons[2], the sisters met Mrs. Hodgson Burnett[3], famous as the creator of Little Lord Fauntleroy, a prolific authoress and literary ally of Kate Riggs. Mary was the reverse of dazzled by this figure and describes in her diary,

[1] Authoress and friend of Kate Riggs.

[2] Robert Underwood Johnson, editor, author, Chevalièr of the Legion of Honour, France, 1891, Cavalière of the Arms of Italy, 1895, Ambassador to Italy, 1920.

[3] Frances Hodgson Burnett wrote the introduction to the Quillcote Edition of Kate Douglas Wiggin's books.

a short, grossly fat woman, with an evil eye, dyed hair dressed low and tied with ribbons, a dirty crushed white gown, very *décolletée* . . .

and the scrutiny proceeds, missing nothing and culminating in 'she was like a nightmare dream'. The few further encounters with Mrs. Hodgson Burnett provoked no comment from the diarist.

The prize for rich vulgarity which both horrified and amused the Findlaters was carried off by another woman whose gilded room they approached by a double staircase. Around part of the chamber ran a small gilt gallery. Seated on a gilt Empire sofa was

a huge, horse-faced, high cheek-boned woman with loose lips and prominent fishy eyes and a rasping voice.

Before her was placed

a tea tray of silver, loaded with silver dishes the very flame of the silver lamp protected by a silver screen. 'What will you have?' she inquired, 'I have the Queen of England's own tea, Persian tea brought over in a sealed casket especially for my-self, Russian tea with lemon or Cherry Bounce – which will you have?' We selected the Queen of England's own tea and were presented each with a small gilt cup of cold mash. As each guest finished and laid down her little doyley, she wiped her own mouth with it or clutched and crumpled it in one of her great hands, and then mashed it into a heap in the corner of the great gilt sofa behind her. She held a hydra-headed electric bell, upon which her fingers played continually, and summoned a different servant every minute, it seemed. Her order sometimes took the form of a forefinger stretched out and pointed. Talk was about the 'Simpler Life'.

They were fascinated by their visit to the Thompson Setons,[1] the sleigh ride from Gascob station, rolled up in rugs, over frozen snow, the house 'much like' the houses at Beer;

[1] Ernest Thompson Seton, naturalist, artist, author, lecturer, b. 1860 d. 1946.

Mrs. Seton's room so full of every luxury, bed built into cornice so that curtains could be drawn round it. Mr. Seton's study with drawers full of hundreds of bird skins; Indian coats and weapons, notes for new book.

The Findlaters' dislike of ostentation or affectation of any kind, intense where vulgarity reinforced wealth, was in other circumstances modified or almost obliterated by amusement as when, after a 'sticky studio tea at Miss Usher's', a

Mr. Laughton insisted on taking us to the room of a friend . . . a madman apparently – hung about with everything from nuts and strings of beads, Indian hammocks, oleographs, parasols, feathers, skulls, bones, banjoes, fringes, canoes, rugs, paper lanterns . . . all covered thick with dust – not a clear inch of space anywhere.

When visiting the Carnegie mansion on a charitable errand, however, their purpose overcame their disgust. Mary then notes both the

sweet summer temperature of the rooms, filled with roses

as well as the

terrible bad taste of the whole house, Mrs. C. quite simple and kind, Mr. Carnegie just as he looked before, not one of Nature's gentlemen,

but he showed himself a kind benefactor, for at the instance of the two Findlaters he took up Mora's delicate, poverty-stricken young protégée, Maggie Taylor, and made her a small allowance for the rest of her brief life. After this, the two went on to visit a couple of ladies in a

small hot apartment entirely filled by a grand piano (Winged Victory as everywhere), they were entertaining a Dutch nobleman (who hastily took his leave) and a young pianist who opened the piano, played violently and then went away.

The sisters were clearly intrigued by Mrs. Strong in her dress 'painted with scarlet poppies', with 'beads and shells and beetles hung all over her', her 'rolling dark eye' and 'warm hand' and her friend Mrs. Norris,

> tight-laced, *décolletée*; small vacant face; lips reddened with paste; dreamy replies, lost in memory of her husband; quite sympathetic: told me she and Mrs. Strong carried about a small idol, and that at first she did not believe in it, but now always made it some small offering before undertaking any plan.

The time in New York was drawing to a close. It was brief enough, but they had seen various facets of the city's life, which, despite some notable exceptions, had left a predominating impression of crudity. The Findlaters were not enthusiastic about the Central Park which, for Henry James, writing a year or two later,[1] possessed a 'sweet ingratiation' even though it failed to achieve the impossible aim of satisfying tastes as innumerable and diverse as the languages spoken within its tiny precincts. 'Small half-grown trees', bluntly comments Mary, 'and little knolls and curly-wurly walks – no attempt at formality – very unimpressive.'

The last Saturday in New York was celebrated by a visit to the theatre. 'A rich friend' of Kate Riggs had lent her box 'for an evening when no one was there.' It was not a happy occasion. The performance of 'Aida' provided the Findlaters with two hours of indescribable boredom, the audience depressed them by its dowdiness, 'everyone in blouses', nor did the company in the box improve matters, two gentlemen and 'a nameless, always bright and grateful woman in black net and beads, very galvanized.' A ballet of negro girls, 'fans – glaring light – mock gorgeousness and squalling voices' added the last touch of horror.

On the following Monday they saw Yeats's *Cathleen ni Houlihan* at the Hudson Theatre, 'exquisite – so badly acted'.

On the first day of March the two ladies set off for Boston. A 'nice telegram' from the warm-hearted Kate greeted them there. Mary immediately sensed the 'genteel atmosphere' of the boarding-house where they were domiciled and within forty-eight hours

[1] Henry James, *The American Scene*, London, 1907, p. 174 et seq.

had summed up the fellow guests with a few crisp, vivid words on each.

The first Sunday of their visit to Boston found Mary and Jane at a 'Christian Science temple with Mrs. Coolidge: a kindly resolute person whom we at once understood'. It was the usual 'huge round building', but this, and the service, were a new experience to the sisters, and, as might have been expected, an alien one.

'How all sense of worship had died out'

exclaims the diarist.

> Contrast one of the high old solemn laborious Churches of the West with this. Their chaste, hard-won solemnity, their stone pillars, flagged floors, grave altars, with the round painted walls, plush carpets, walnut wood decorations . . . pots of flowers in common green glaze, footstools, arm-chairs, desks.

All of a piece were the

> fat, smooth-faced, low-voiced, clean-shaven young man with a plump white hand, reading from one desk the precepts of Mrs. Eddy, just like a cat that has been licking cream, a tense shrivelled woman in black with her hair screwed into a knot at the back of her head reading the much less attractive fragments from the Bible

and

> Mrs. Eddy's precepts painted on the walls.

> It was strange to find the compositions of none other than Aunt Jane Borthwick in the Hymnary.

> Crowded house, awful trivialities and dullness of service 'Our Father and Mother God',

are Mary's concluding remarks on that Sunday's experiences.

The luncheons, teas and dinners continued. Mary confesses to feeling 'Swiftian', which for her and Jane signified a black mood of destructive criticism and disgust. An expedition to Concord 'through wooden villages' proved a pleasant interlude. They were met by Miss Jane Perkins and brought back to her old house which seemed filled by the pleasantly familiar smell of peat and wood smoke. There were shabby, antique pieces of furniture, four-poster beds, 'lovely little pictures' and most important of all 'books to the roof' and talk of books ('our own books loved here', interpolated Mary), of Scotland, of politics, until luncheon was served in a 'tiny dining-room off priceless old blue china. Not a flower on the table. Coarse clean linen.' Afterwards they went out in sleighs over frozen snow, through pine trees and 'peace' to see the 'Emerson House' and 'Alcott House' and the celebrated graveyard, a high mound covered with frozen snow, where rested the mortal remains of the Concord philosophers and writers, their famous names, a galaxy still shining with un-dimmed splendour in 1905, unshadowed as yet by the clouds of fashion and taste which have since passed over them. They saw the bridge across the stream; the soldier's monument and, down to earth once more, returned to tea with Miss Perkins, 'evidently unaccustomed but so good', then back to the 'tiny station, almost like a private house where everyone knew everyone else, and where and why they were going'.

The Findlaters returned to a round of luncheons, teas and dinners, but they carried with them Miss Perkins' assurance, 'there will be one door open for you in New England' and were to pay other visits to her 'old house' with its dark rooms 'like Ann Street' and to have there more delightful converse, drink more 'good cups of tea' and hear her reiterated, 'If you ever need a friend, and in a new country one sometimes does, come to me, you have one here.'

They enjoyed driving with Miss Pingree in her smart carriage with fur rugs, and the luncheon to which she took them at the Mayflower Club. Other drives were less agreeable, 'long and dull' like the luncheons with a lady whom Mary found

so suggestive of Aunt Robina; painted, powdered, resolute to talk of higher things; rooms crammed with tasteless pseudo-culture, plush, Italian photographs and so on.

The Swiftian mood was on once more: 'Jane again trying to curb me and be amiable,' notes Mary, but

'I knew what the house would be like before I went in; the doorsteps told me, and the fierce clutch of the woman who took us in a cab – result of a mistaken moment of sympathy about her spine.'

Mary now determined that she must try to be more like their friend Margaret Roberton, with her even disposition and cheerful, consistent interest in everything. The new resolution, however, failed to enhance 'the frescoes in the Library', of Longfellow's 'mansion' Mary noted, 'white antimacassars – the poet's bust everywhere: the obvious always; cheerful sunny rooms,' but immediately in the next note the tone changes. Briefly Mary records: 'Met Colonel Higginson'[1] and quotes:

Or ever the knightly years had gone
With the old world to the grave,

adding 'such a touching old idealist, so brave and gentle, so untrimmed and so ill-shod compared to our men'.

Yet briefer and more restrained is the allusion which follows to the beginning of one of the deepest and most lasting friendships of the two sisters' experience:

Met Mrs. William James and knew her for a friend.

The round of entertainment continued.

Out at night to dine with Mrs. Loring. Wandering . . . in the dark . . . streets we missed our way and scuttled about until we were both quite tired – then at last arrived – found I had brought no shoes. Borrowed a new pair from the maid. Mrs. Deland and Mrs. Schelseiger the only guests – interesting talk. Sat in the dark looking out on the great river with blocks of drifting ice slowly floating down – lights reflected on the ice – long line of crimson still in the sky – one star and crescent moon

[1] Thomas Wentworth Higginson, author, who lived at 29 Buckingham St., Camb. Mass.

also reflected palely in the ice below. Talked of the future life. Mrs. Deland told us about her presentiment under ether about Mr. Mackinley's assassination. Mrs. S. drove us home. Discreetly admitted by Miss MacHugo.

Mary would not have missed that little concluding touch of Victorian propriety.

On 15th March they

set out early driven by Mrs. Putnam to a luncheon-party at Miss Amy Lowell's huge house 'semi-country' a good deal of 'old servant' and 'grandfather', large party, elaborate meal. Miss Lowell hugely fat, shaking with shrill laughter -- not as old as ourselves . . . Sat on comfortable sofa before large wood fire and thought 'Oh! if I might only have two hours of rest here with a book.'

But a tea-party was awaiting them, another somewhat wearisome affair, and the tea itself 'cold wash' though Miss Pingree's presence was stimulating and 'delightful.'

It was during this week that they went to see Mrs. Julia Ward Howe. They had heard a rather fulsome admirer describe that veteran authoress, pioneer of Women's Rights and bard of the famous 'Battle Hymn of the Republic' as 'Old!, No!, the youngest thing in America!'

The diarist writes:

We were shown upstairs and found 'the youngest thing in America' a very ancient lady[1] seated on a chair in the centre of her drawing-room, holding a sort of court. She was dressed in sea-green surah with rich falls of very cotton cotton lace, and wore a small round cap. She appeared quite dull and uninterested in anything.

Several second-rate looking young literary men were hovering about, and some dull women kept coming and going. A niece was chattering in a corner.

It is clear that despite strictures, criticisms and some confessions

[1] Mrs. Julia Ward Howe, b. 1819, d. 1910.

of boredom, both sisters (like many travellers from these islands before and since) found in Boston and Cambridge a human environment far more agreeable than New York, although, in the great city, as at home in London, Jane appeared to wilt much less than Mary, who used to tell me that while she always became exhausted and destroyed by town life, it suited Jane.

In the middle of March the prospect had brightened and joyfully expanded with an invitation from Mrs. William James to stay with her at Cambridge. The attraction at first sight had been mutual. Alice James told her husband that she intended to invite the authoresses to come on a visit. He suggested that this was a little incautious on so brief an acquaintance. She assured him that the arrangement would be successful. She had no doubts as to the kind of women her future guests were. Mary and Jane had accepted the invitation with alacrity and looked forward to seeing Mrs. William James again with happy anticipation.

At the William James's they felt completely at home. He was away when they arrived, but when eventually the sisters met him, the intangible link was forged, almost as swiftly as it had been with his wife. The Findlaters felt perfectly happy with her and with her mother, Mrs. Gibbons (who was with her daughter at the time of their visit), especially as the ladies sat together discussing anything in heaven or earth, in a big, low book-lined room, with a huge writing-table (William's) at the end of it, and a 'statue in the corner – so virile and beautiful'. Mary and Jane delighted in 'the home life' which surrounded them, 'the boys' and their friends coming and going. They appreciated the simple meals, especially the arrangements on Sunday when guests could help themselves from plain but excellent cold fare left for them on the sideboard. The atmosphere was entirely congenial.

On the second day of their visit Mrs. James took her friends over to tea with the Nortons, Mary notes the

old rather gloomy house set in pine wood; pools of water with pines standing in them . . . dark rooms full of very old furniture; gentle-mannered very pleasing women.

Professor Charles Eliot Norton at that time in his seventy-ninth year, was their host. George Santayana described him as 'a most urbane and exquisite spirit . . . descended from a long line of typical New England divines'. A Frenchman, who knew him intimately, put him down as a 'terrible Yankee'.[1] Mary saw an 'old man with a red face and watery eyes – gentle cultivated manner' who brought them 'into his study; dark room lined with books and with picture in gorgeous old carved gilt Venetian frame.'

Even while the Findlaters stayed with Mrs. James, the round of luncheons, teas and dinners closed in upon them. Miss Sally Norton accompanied them when they dined at the Edward Robinsons'[2] where the dinner-table was covered from end to end with roses to honour *The Rose of Joy*.

It was quaintly appropriate that a snow-storm preceded the appearance upon the scene on 21st March of Miss Ellen Emerson. Her father, Ralph Waldo Emerson, had welcomed her at her birth on 24th February, 1839, as his 'Winter bud'.[3] Now, at sixty-six, she was supported by crutches and seemed to Mary's eyes a somewhat formidable old lady.

In the estimate of most contemporaries, and especially of Americans, Miss Emerson was naturally enough surrounded by mists of sentiment, almost a halo, for she had been since girlhood the dedicated pillar of her parents' household, the ever-competent manager of her brothers with all their comings and goings the prop of her revered and eminent Father's old age and pathetically

[1] *George Santayana, Character and opinion in the United States,* London, 1920, pp. 141-2. Professor Norton is also described here as 'the friend of Carlyle, of Burne-Jones, and of Matthew Arnold'. It was he who advised Bernard Berenson, the future eminent authority on Italian Renaissance and pre-renaissance art, against reading Walter Pater, and was largely responsible for preventing Harvard from buying Italian primitives, which, as the Jarves Collection, eventually became the glory of Yale v. Sylvia Sprigge, *Berenson*, London, 1950.

[2] Mr. Edward Robinson had been Lecturer on Classical Archaeology at Harvard, and became distinguished in the Archaeological and Museum world throughout Europe and America.

[3] *Journals of Ralph Waldo Emerson* 1838-41, ed. Edward Waldo Emerson and Waldo Emerson Forbes, London, 1911.

failing memory. She was indeed an individual, a remarkable person, and as such, aroused directly in Mary half amused, but wholly sincere, regard.

The diarist briefly sketches in Miss Emerson's 'purple cloth dress', her 'white hair brushed flat to the head, serious simple fine face', and adds that she 'made one see how much of the dullness of conversation came from not speaking the truth'. The purple cloth was exchanged for 'willow green silk at night' and the never-idle fingers were employed with 'a bit of coarse knitting, I saw her counting my feet,' continues Mary,

> as I sat with one foot under me. Her household, consisting of 'the two forties, the two sixties and the two nineties' at Concord rises every morning at half-past four or five – generally in bed by eight. When we asked her if she never felt time long she replied, 'there are always trunks to sort'.

Mary's brief and sole comment here was: 'she had the look of one who had lived by a closed door, I thought, seeing Mrs. James and her boys beside her'.

On the following day, 22nd March, the Diary continues:

> Went with Mrs. James to a luncheon-party at Mrs. Putnam's. Miss Emerson had set off early, a piece of brown paper tied over her bonnet by a black handkerchief 'nothing so preserves the feather from damp'. She sat at the luncheon-table calm and majestic, the only person there without a bonnet, enjoying the foods she liked and rejecting those she didn't with the simplicity of a child. We were seated between two wearisome women and could look across at Mrs. James's face with her great dark eyes, longing to have been talking to her. After lunch I made a frantic effort to be pleasant with the result that another weariful woman tacked herself on to us all the way home . . . Mrs. James had a tea-party in the afternoon. . .

Here another female 'bore', a 'Biblical Lecturer', filled the sisters with amused dismay by announcing that she considered 'Heaven meant spending Eternity with those who attracted you, she', adds the diarist, 'had decided to spend it with us'.

Next day at a small luncheon-party given for the Findlaters by their hostess, conversation turned upon Mrs. Piper, 'the woman with four personalities', a subject of particular interest to the William Jameses.[1] At a later date, when Mary asked Mr. James why the messages of mediums often seemed so childishly silly, he illustrated his conjecture as to the reason by the analogy of a situation in which a message had to be entrusted to a drunken man.[2] Mary frequently alluded to the delight of conversation with William James, and how by him, even the stumbling of lesser intellects and the suggestions of the inexpert were turned to some fruitful or significant discussion. To the truly questing mind his strong intellect gave an exhilarating stimulus. There was 'no subject in heaven or earth', so Henry James once remarked to Mary, that William and his wife would not tackle 'in the space of furling or unfurling their umbrellas'.

The sisters could have remained happily in this fascinating and congenial company, but an urgent and pressing invitation had been given them by the Houghtons[3] which they felt it incumbent upon them to accept. Sadly and reluctantly they packed 'in deep gloom . . . almost in despair,' but later in the day they were cheered by luncheon in Boston with Margaret Deland. Then having said good-bye to Mrs. William James, they set off for the Houghtons.

Both ladies were too weary to appreciate the German play they were taken to see on their first evening, but they were enchanted by their visit to the Riverside Press on the following morning and

[1] Mrs. Piper was a celebrated American medium, v. William James, *Final Impressions of a Psychical Researcher and Report on Mrs. Piper's Hodgson-Control* in *Proceedings of the Eng. Society for Psychical Research.* 1909 and *Proc. of Am. Soc. for Psychical Research,* 1909.

[2] Cp. William James, *Final Impressions of a Psychical Researcher* in *Memories and Studies,* London, 1911, p. 203, where he writes that his friend, Richard Hodgson of Cambridge, used to 'liken the difficulties to those of two persons who on earth should have only dead-drunk servants to use as their messengers'.

[3] Henry O. Houghton, Mifflin & Co. Publishers.

especially delighted with the marbling paper work'. The tea- and dinner-party which followed were also enjoyable; the chief guests were a Mr. and Mrs. Kay:

Mr. Kay so typically Scotch singing *When the Kye Come Hame*. Mrs. Kay so kind, beautifully dressed, talking much of brides; three daughters just married. She gave an account of a party at Mr. Emerson's[1] which she had attended as a girl. They danced and danced until the dust flew up from the floor – still danced on – then Mr. Emerson went off to bed, and huge baskets were brought in containing fresh crackers, jugs of cold water. She said nothing ever tasted so good.

The parties continued varied by an expedition to see 'Mrs. Gardner's Palace'[2] built in Venetian style containing, 'Priceless treasures of art within – gaping crowds of tourists'.

Mary's further comment upon 'one of the finest art galleries which has been open to the public'[2] is characteristic of an eye which enjoyed violent and significant contrast;

from the very window [she continues] by which hung the Botticelli picture, you looked out on a dreary litter of garbage, old tin cans, papers, refuse of all sorts and marshy pools of stagnant water. One young man amongst the crowd with lovely Italian profile.

In 1905 the 'haunting presence' had not yet come to dominate her Venetian palace of Fenway Court[3] or the sisters might have reacted to the atmosphere as they did to the much more sinister associations of Salem, which they visited on 28th March (Mary's fortieth birthday) with Mrs. Kershaw and Alberta Houghton.

Where Henry James's impressions weave and interweave like the delicate filaments of a spider's web[4] there was for Mary one

[1] Ralph Waldo Emerson.

[2] *Who's Who in America.* For accounts of Isabella Stewart Gardner v. Ellery Sidgwick, *The Happy Profession,* Boston, 1946 and Morris Carter, *Isabella Stewart Gardner, London,* 1926.

[3] Roger Hinks and Naomi Royde-Smith, *Pictures and People,* Gollancz, 1930.

[4] Henry James, *The American Scene,* London, 1907, p. 265 et seq.

inescapable thought. The place was witch-haunted. She who loved
the grace of ancient buildings and looked upon old furniture with
the eye of a connoisseur, found 'the old part of the town hideous'
and notes,

old blackened tumbledown timber buildings with yards filled
with rubbish. Hawthorne's[1] birthplace, a grim house in a sordid
street. The House of the Seven Gables, a small rather dilapidated timber house with low gables standing close to the shore.
You could squeeze through the fence beside the garden, and
stand looking out on the old Harbour and the Bay. The Custom
House with wooden pillars at the door, and an open space leading down to the sea in front; great squalor everywhere. The old
Witch House now a Druggist's Shop, very low in the roof, and
almost pitch-dark within. Smell of drugs and groceries. I asked
the man if he had seen any ghosts, and he laughed at the idea.

The Court House containing all the MS accounts of the
various trials for witchcraft, still in the old faded writing, too
horrible and pitiful to read. Card of witch pins, evil looking
little twisted metal pins, declared to have been found in the flesh
of the bewitched.

A shadow, to me, hung over the whole town. In one of the
busiest streets a tablet is erected which records how on this
spot a man was condemned for witchcraft, imprisoned and
'afterwards pressed to death'. Just after reading it we saw an
old crazed woman wander past in the crowd with such a dreadful and malign face. Doubtless such scenes had had a terrible
influence upon the next generation. Then saw the little shed
that now covers the remaining timbers of Salem Chapel. Above
the door a little picture of an old English Country Church.

Then drove in to the better part of the town and saw a lovely
old colonial house of the 'Adams' period with doorways
arranged with the most delicate traceries over glass, and slender,

[1] Nathaniel Hawthorne, novelist, b. Salem, Massachusetts 1804, d.1864.
Author of *The Scarlet Letter*, 1850; *The House of the Seven Gables*, 1851, and
many other novels and stories.

classic white pillars. A broad street of them shaded with trees. Then to lunch at the Club in Salem – another of those delightful old houses. Wide, stately exquisitely proportioned rooms, shallow open staircases with delicate balustrades, old chimney-pieces, old furniture here and there – sunny, cheerful altogether charming. Wandered about a little looking at shops. Back to hideous new station.

Out to a Shakespeare reading in the evening. A small drawing-room so packed with people that once seated you couldn't move. The last act of *The Tempest* was read. Then a man read a long original composition, a sort of continuation of *The Tempest* bringing in all the well-known characters, Hamlet, Lear, Othello and so on. He afterwards was introduced to me and apologized for not having introduced Portia as he had 'already at another time written a continuation to *The Merchant of Venice*'. He seemed quite unembarrassed.

When they returned to New York at the end of the month it was to stay at the Smalley's with whose way of life they were obviously more at home than with that of the Riggs Household.

We noticed how smart all the men appeared after Cambridge. The fresh air and refinement of the Smalley's house *very* refreshing.

After a day of crowded shopping or a visit to Chinatown, fascinating in its way, but with 'awful mingled smells that smote you suddenly from the cellars', it was restoring to return to Evelyn's room with its pink-shaded lamps, its photographs and pictures of interesting people, for a quiet talk.

The Smalleys and the Riggs gathered at the station to see Mary and Jane off for Arkansas. The two settled down in their little state-room then watched from the windows as they went up the Hudson.

Their final destination was Clover Bend, the home of Miss Alice French, a lady more widely known as Octave Thanet, the authoress of many books, mainly novels. 'You have always been my literary master,' she once wrote to William Dean Howells. 'I am as uncompromising a realist as lives'.[1]

From Mary Findlater's accounts, and later in the Diary as well, one receives an impression not only of Miss French's forceful, calm capability, but also of the latent energy and power which brought her, in her sixties, to the forefront as a local administrator and leader in women's organizations during the 1914–18 War, a calamity which was still nine years and more ahead on this April morning, and as yet cast no shadow of coming disaster across the minds of ordinary people. Nor was it sensed by many of the less ordinary, such as the pair clattering along in the train through strange and fascinating scenery.

On Friday, 7th, they were passing

farms, farms – lonely bits of wood and scattered towns, fields covered with snow, bare trees, desolate landscape. Came into St. Louis late at night, across the river sparkling with lights. Warmer again. Huge new station with staircase running up to the waiting-room, dome-like mosque with great painted roof. People sitting everywhere. A woman with her baby sleeping beside her stretched out sound asleep on the floor of the waiting room. Stalls where Indians sold Indian and Mexican wares, leavings of the 'World's Fair'. Rubber pavement that made no noise to the feet.

Dark warm night air. Got into another train. Negro conductor. Very talkative. Woke in the morning to warmth and sun. Green rivers, trees covered with bright pink blossoms reflected in the pale green water.

Towards evening the train began to pass through cypress swamps,

glittering pools amongst the trees, lean white cows feeding here and there. Arrived at Hoxie at ten o'clock. Descended from the train by a wooden stool. It drifted on and we were left to do as best we could. Two old railway carriages set on

[1] Edwin H. Candy, *The Realist at War. The Mature Years 1885–1920 of William Dean Howells,* Syracuse Univ. Press, 1958, p. 211.

end, one marked 'White Waiting Room' the other 'Coloured Waiting Room'. A few battered wooden huts; two houses marked 'Saloons'. A house with a balcony marked 'Pool', a long bit of wooden sidewalk straggling down on one side. Huge filthy black pigs routing everywhere. A car drawn by one tiny thin old mule, the reins hitched to the roof to spare trouble to the driver, came slowly along the line; two men rode up in green embroidered Mexican gauntlets.

We sat on the hotel veranda where it was desperately hot, and saw a fat Negro waiter in broken shoes and with a face marked by small-pox blacken the boots of a broken down white man, who first gave a wave of the hand to show what he wanted. Oppressive silence everywhere. Knots of men sitting about on doorsteps or logs. The only things that moved were the black Porter and the little mule.

We could see in the room behind us a man making up accounts and two or three other men sitting with their feet on the table. There seemed to be a good deal of business in the Hotel. People came and went in silence; once a train passed and a young man and a woman in a huge feathered hat got out and assisted by the Porter, vanished into the Hotel. We got out and walked down the sidewalk, passed a building that still had the sign 'Drug Store' . . . some loafers hardly moved to let us pass. A cow eating wood. A house where a woman in a cotton dressing-gown was lounging about. We went into a store and bought some 5 cent studs. Came back and waited again in the heat until at last our train came up. Got in along with a crowd of people who had mysteriously appeared. Some people got out – an old man and a very old woman with a thin brown face who was quite dazed. She came on slowly from behind and was met by a tall Scotch-looking young man carrying a child on his shoulder, who seized her hand, calling out 'Who's this, Mother? Who's this?' She began to scream out 'It's Donald!' laughing vaguely – and we got into the train. There was a little boy carrying a large green parrot in such a small cage that it had to sit on its own tail.

The little scene on Hoxie platform was a gift to a Victorian novelist or story-teller. Jane used it in her *Charlie Over the Water*,[1] and Ruth Draper had such an incident in her repertoire.

On went the train

slowly through the swamps to Portia, a small village where we again disembarked on the wooden stool. A man in a soft hat with a flat face and thin grey beard introduced himself as Colonel Tucker, and handed a note from Miss French. We got into a phaeton with two rough young horses and drove for nine miles along roads formed entirely of sand. The sun was burning hot and the road quite unshaded. We had had no food since breakfast except a bit of chocolate. Fields of green corn, cotton fields like rows of little sticks, small wooden houses everywhere around the clearings, the dense forest.

Reached Clover Bend and drove up a little newly laid out garden to a grey, painted wooden house with a dazzling white veranda. In front of the house were beds of brilliant flowers and trees covered with lilac blossom. Huge butterflies, some jet black, fluttered everywhere. Scarlet cardinal birds with a lovely note flew among the bushes. There was a green rushing river at the side, more fields of cotton, everywhere in the distance the wall of the forest.

Inside, the house was like a comfortable shooting lodge, polished floors, rugs, white curtains, white furniture, gauze screens over every door and window. Miss French in white piqué. Mrs. Crawford in grey linen. Hot water, tea, scented soaps, comfortable beds – all perfectly charming.

Sat out on the veranda and looked about and heard the cardinal birds singing above us. Miss French introduced . . . a thick set, rather bow-legged young man, as 'Mr. Drake, the Plantation Manager'. Then Colonel Tucker came in to dinner, having previously apologized for having no dress-clothes with him. He was a silent man with a flat, inexpressive face. Indeed they were all silent.

[1] Jane H. Findlater, *Seven Scots Stories,* London, 1912.

After dinner we all sat out of doors again in the darkness. The whole horizon was instantly lit up by sheet lightning. A banjo was played in one of the Negro cabins across the river, frogs made a singing almost like some queer bird in the cypress swamps. When you walked out on the grass it was perfectly dry. Colonel Tucker told me a story about his brother. He had been riding for a whole long day somewhere in Texas, and came after dark to one of the log huts put up for travellers, called and got no answer, dismounted, rubbed down his horse, entered the hut and rolled himself up on the floor. Woke in the grey light of early morning to find three dead men hanging from the beam above his bed.

On Sunday, 9th April, the heat became intense. It was possible only to walk 'a little bit in the morning'. Later in the afternoon they

watched a Negro breaking in a mule. There was an old mule harnessed into a heavy cart, an animal so sly and aged that nothing the other did could move it for an instant. It . . . stepped across the pole into its own place and stood there im-movable whilst the young one kicked and plunged. Mr. Drake came to dinner.

Thus the days went by. They gathered mushrooms, and watched from the shelter of the house, great and magnificent thunderstorms. They drove with two mules, far into the forest or 'dug about the Indian mounds in the fields with Mr. Drake and a Negro but got nothing'.

On one occasion they had

luncheon in the forest on benches provided for a Negro Preach-ing. Then dug again fruitlessly. Some Negro women 'came silently out of the wood' mutely asking for food. Miss French gave them oranges and sweets and remains of food. Some were selling thread for which they got a copper.

On Friday, 14th April, they had another

long drive in the forest passing into the exquisite green glade where the grass was like emeralds. Two Negroes went with us and dug in the Indian mounds.

Silence of the black men. Mr. Drake riding up and tying his smoking horse to a little tree. The child's grave covered with rough logs. The drive afterwards through the trees, winding in and out and crashing through the thorn bushes, the horses jumping over logs in the path. Drove round by the Cane Brake, delicate pointed leaves on slender stems. Cattle browsing amongst it. Little lonely tent in the woods where, Mr. Drake told us, he once found a young man cowering. He asked him what he was doing there and all the young man would answer was 'If you won't let me stay here I will go and find a hollow tree and die there.' Mr. Drake left him and went for a team of mules and a cart, but when they got there the hut was empty, and they never found any trace of him again.

Beside the sandy road leading to Miss French's gate there was a store about which there always seemed to be gathered a group of men. There was 'a broad cheerful space in front' and it was situated opposite Colonel Tucker's house,

another smaller white-painted wooden house with a low veranda, absolutely overhung and darkened by huge masses of creeper. No gardens there, none of the brightness of Miss French's. The Plantation had come to Mrs. Crawford through her father. One of his ancestors when turned out to the war had confided to a faithful servant where he had buried his treasure, but the man too was killed and the treasure is still there. Black pigs routing about everywhere. Wild dogs in the forest summoned by a horn to be fed, but the man did not have to dismount.

There was a spit of white sand on the river opposite our windows, and the old Negroes said they remembered the panthers coming out there 'to play like kittens in the sun'. Sometimes, early in the morning before it was light, you could hear the whistle of a steamer and then, hours afterwards, for the curve made by the river was so great, a queer high-decked steamer came slowly nosing round the corner. People on board did washing and all their parti-coloured clothes were drying on lines on the deck. There seemed no reason for its coming and going. The small boats were almost flat like rafts, with a curve at the prow.

We had sucking pig at dinner one evening, carried by a Negro on a great dish. It held a lemon in its mouth and was trimmed about with garlands of pink honeysuckle.

On Saturday, 16th April, there were

athletic sports in the afternoon on the ground, in front of the store.

Quite a crowd of people. Women with babies about ten days old. Girls in blouses and huge transparent hats. A knot of Negroes standing by themselves watching, not allowed to join in.

Miss French 'moved about among them keeping order'. She carried in one hand a beautiful white handkerchief. Beneath its folds, (so Mary told me) she concealed a small revolver.

Lean, long nosed men in all kinds of clothes with brown faces and slouch hats, some with bare feet, all jostling fiercely and disputing about almost every race. Very clumsy in movement and not well made. The prizes were given by Miss French. One was a water jug and basin in which were placed several cakes of soap. This was much desired. Shirts and a watch were also given. The men complained of heat and were breathless even after a short run.

We sat on chairs in a wagon. The wind was very cold and the small babies began to cry.

On Sunday they packed and then

. . . walked about with Mrs. Crawford and Mr. Drake looking for arrow-heads in the white sand of the roads where the rain had washed a channel.

When they went into the pasture and the wood behind they saw two cardinal birds hopping on the ground where they appeared absurdly fine.

Vines grew up the trees to the very top and then flung themselves down in ropes and garlands.

The beautiful trim condition of everything about the house and garden was a lesson in that wilderness; a light in a dark place; probably the one civilizing influence in that locality.

Early in the morning of Monday, 17th April, Mary and Jane left Clover Bend in a carriage with luncheon baskets, driven by a Negro. They took a road other than that by which they had come.

Crossed some curious long bridges, past many lonely farms, and little old farm-houses, with the beams jointed instead of nailed together. Stopped outside Hoxie and took lunch in the carriage, then drove over the worst bit of road we had yet seen, deep pits, hummocks of sand, mud that the horses could scarcely drag the carriage through.

Again waited an hour at Hoxie. This time went into the hotel. Saw two strange bedrooms on the ground floor, the ricketty walls seemed no thicker than paste board, the beds low and dirty, the rooms so unprotected that you felt anything might happen in them, they were very large. The sitting-room had a stove burning full blast, and every breath of air excluded, so that it was scarcely possible to stay in it for one minute. Two young women, one dressed in crimson cashmere and holding a baby, were rocking in rocking chairs by the stove, though the temperature outside was that of a summer day. The wooden walls were covered with strange, cheap flaring paper. They appeared talking with a kind of listless mystery, so that you wondered what they were doing there at all.

The landlady was a buxom young woman who lived in a room with a bow window far on the other side of the hotel. We saw that the Negro waiter had apparently got new clothes, *a gentleman's good boots too,* since we were there before. One wondered where the owner of the boots was now.

As we left Hoxie we looked at the lower windows protected

by iron bars and 'Pool' written on the gable. A group of tawdry women and two men were gathered on the balcony, hanging over to watch the train.

The train was dreadfully hot; very fat man lay on one of the mats near me and sang aloud to himself nearly the whole time.

More of the endless cypress swamps – cabins – Negroes, the buildings becoming more and more utterly dilapidated and tumbledown as we went further South. 'Saloon' at every siding. 'Open all night', generally a Barber's shop too . . . overdressed moustached evil-looking men standing by the door. Cabins standing in the water mounted on high piles to keep above the swamp, Negresses in brilliant and grotesque clothes, scarcely human in appearance, pink, scarlet, bright blue dresses, huge flimsy fashionable hats with white spotted veils standing all round their black faces. A cabin in a wood with a huge Negress at the door, in a pink tea-gown.

A dead cow lying by the railway line – killed by the train. A group of other cattle feeding quite undisturbed beside it.

Suddenly in the uncared for country a white man's Club, for sportsmen, all painted in and out, spick and span with tidy grounds. Wolves in the forest behind, they told us. Saw furniture of a small house, evidently just bought which had all been cast out from wagons down the railway bank and left for the owners to secure. Everything broken and knocked about, the new iron bedstead thrown into the road, the small zinc bath bashed in, the poor little tables and chairs and rolls of linoleum pitched together down the bank. Negro families coming out at every station.

The travellers arrived at Memphis in 'hot twilight'. There Miss French's friend, Dr. Minor, was waiting for them and drove them 'through huge dilapidated streets, full of coloured people, broken fences, ill-kept roadways. General air of utter stagnation and unkemptness.'

Eventually the party arrived at a small house standing on a

steep bank where they were received by Mrs. Minor in white silk and were

led through square Hall decorated in the Baronial style, upstairs to a smelling bathroom with no hot water, gas escaping, family nailbrush, scraped paint, every evidence of poverty; then into a large bedroom with windows tight shut, and furnace on full blast. Gas escaping there too, grit everywhere, atmosphere particularly stifling. Bed in an alcove, apart from the rest of the room.

Downstairs a small room off the Hall. Every window closed and large fire burning. Small niece, also in white, with dark hair and large, dark eyes.

She was a Southern girl, in Memphis to 'come out'.

Sat making conversation till dinner was announced,

and then they were regaled on

black butter, anchovies on toast, soup, lobster, hot rolls, fried chicken, pineapple salad, veal cutlets with tinned green peas, iced punch, sweets, ice-cream decorated with roses in honour of *The Rose of Joy*. Very sour strawberries, coffee, dessert.

After dinner was over, again returned to sit and converse in suffocating parlour. Nearly fell asleep, exhausted almost to tears. Discussed the Negroes with Mrs. Minor who told us they spoke to animals exactly as if they were their equals and that animals won't pay the slightest heed to them if there are white people there. Told us she had invited twenty people to meet us that evening, but her husband had obliged her to telephone and put them off.

Glimpses of society in Memphis, 'house party', 'culture' and so on. Literary society had discussed our books. Drove back along the dark, untidy, jumbled streets in the hot darkness. Got on board the train about eleven. Very sleepy and quite comfortable all night. Awoke early and looked out. Saw glimpses of green country, Negroes, farms. The cypress swamps disappeared and the country became tidier. Passed through wooded, hilly country full of memorials of the War. Here and there a lonely tombstone amongst the woods, or a pillar to show where a battle had been fought. Got very bad food all day . . . Another night in our little berths.

The sisters woke early as they came in to Washington about six o'clock that April morning. They drove from the train, in a cab, through streets lined with trees, exquisitely green in the brilliant sunshine, 'people already hurrying about.' Later in the day they went for an hour's drive, to look about them, and Mary noted,

. . . lovely wide streets lined with green trees, magnolias in full bloom in every garden, wide, gay parks, beautiful public buildings. Motors whizzing everywhere, carrying young and interesting people. Exquisite cheerfulness of it all. Washington's Pillar, huge and tall, without the smallest ornament of any kind. *Size* again the criterion. Small vehicle with a linen awning over the top instead of an ordinary cab.

On the following afternoon, Mary and Jane went to tea with the Hitchcocks in their

large cool shady house, with a delightful air of things going on. A very nice girl with a pale face, dark hair and blue eyes, gave us tea, told us she had just been reading *The Rose of Joy* to her sister who was undergoing a rest cure upstairs. Her mother came in, very pale and wearied looking, but sweet too. Father was Secretary for the Interior but had been Ambassador to Russia.[1] The girl had been there. Saw huge, nearly life-size photograph of Mr. Roosevelt in the Library. She said she had liked Mr. McKinley still better.

Next day, Miss Hitchcock came early with her pair of 'swift horses' and 'comfortable carriage' to take the sisters through

[1] Ethan Allan Hitchcock, b. Mobile, Ala., 19th September 1835, d. 1909. Ambassador to Russia, 1898, appointed Secretary of Interior by President McKinley 21st December, 1898, reappointed 5th March, 1901. Remained by request of President Roosevelt, 14th September, 1901, and was reappointed by him. Home St. Louis Residence 1601 K.St., N.W. Washington. V. *Who's Who in America*, 1910.

'lovely bright streets' for a drive. They visited the Capitol, went in and saw the Council Chambers which, remarks Mary,

> were entirely tasteless, full of Cook's tourists, with a guide.
>
> Then on to the White House . . . Cheerful simple rooms, blue drawing-room; a ballroom with cut crystal chandeliers and reflecting mirrors, white halls and pillars, pots of plants, bright sunshine, life and gaiety. Again crowds of tourists, which we escaped by getting into one of the rooms not open to the public. Miss Hitchcock much liked by everyone evidently. She then drove us back to Connecticutt Ave. and we went to a luncheon-party at a Miss Aldis's. Very pretty corner house, large low rooms full of sunshine, flowers, books and old furniture.

Among the guests here was a Mrs. Hobson 'who runs Negro schools in Norfolk' and after lunch there was much talk about the 'Negro Problem', Mrs. Hobson's schools and 'the way that white men insulted the Negro women'.

The Findlaters left Washington on 22nd April. As their train neared New York they watched in fascinated horror as the 'frightful' advertisements spread out before them,

> nineteen life-sized wooden cows in a row in a green field with the figure of a boy on a stool milking one, each cow bearing a letter of 'Harrock's Malted Milk'. Then the winking advertisement that changed as you looked at it from 'So and So's Soups' 'Mix a little hot water and drink.'

They were delighted to arrive at

> the Smalley's door. Delicious welcome. Clean fresh air in the house . . .

On Easter Day (23rd April), the sisters

> made a vain attempt to go to St. Thomas's Church. Crowd too great to attempt to get seats. People shouldering and pushing by hundreds. Ushers useless. Silver trumpets blown in the Church. Flowers being carried or carted all about the streets, many tied up with sort of sashes of blue and pink ribbon or

scarves of chiffon. Home to find a crimson rose given to Evelyn tied with crimson ribbon.

The Smalleys had invited Mr. William Dean Howells[1] and 'his pretty daughter' to meet their guests at luncheon.
Mary notes:

He very common looking, stout and plain with white hair. She like an angel in a picture, with the loveliest smile and expression.

With this champion of Realism[2] the ladies discussed Romance, 'a delightful talk', so the diarist records, and she continues:

Mr. Howells said as he went away, 'Don't say nothing romantic ever happens to you. I am going to put you both into a book, and it's going to make my fortune, and don't you call that romantic?'

The end of their stay in New York was filled with shoppings, commissions and small engagements such as are apt to pile themselves on to the last days of a visit. Miss Mildred Howells came to see them again and presented them with an Indian arrow-head. Packing had to be done in a hustle.

The house seemed strewn with boxes and paper and clothes, and we had to haul nearly everything down three flights of stairs ... We did not change and felt very grubby all evening.

Into this scene, at 'about half-past nine at night', walked 'Mr. Henry James'. It was the Findlaters' first meeting with him. Mary describes

a small, rather stout, clean-shaven man, with a sensitive face. He kissed Evelyn twice, talked nervously, in a great hurry, passing his hand always over his eyes – all about California, *his*

[1] American poet and novelist, b. 1837, d. 1919. The daughter who was with him on this occasion was, presumably, Miss Mildred Howells, herself a writer.

[2] V. Edwin H. Candy, op. cit., p. 194.

lecture to 900 Ladies of Culture, his princely entertainment in a Hotel, where they refused to let him pay the bill.

The day of departure was 26th April. Mary and Jane left the Smalleys early, Evelyn accompanying them. Nora Smith met them at the docks. Mrs. Smalley turned up 'panting and dishevelled' later on. 'Huge crowd', notes the diarist;

> waited about till perfectly exhausted. Then came up to wave to Nora and Evelyn still standing on the wharf, and the ship sailed at last. Flowers everywhere in hampers, bouquets, boxes, stacked unclaimed in the saloon. Went down to unpack and found boxes of sweets sent by our first friend Mrs. Painter[1] with a card, 'Good-bye and come back soon to the finest country on God's earth'.

The American tour was over. The sisters returned on the *Baltic*. On board were also the Carnegies who invited Mary and Jane to share their table with them at meals. This the Findlaters enjoyed, for they found Mrs. Carnegie 'a sweet kind woman', the daughter like her mother, and both, 'simple, natural people'. Mr. Carnegie was, in the Findlaters' estimation, 'blunt and unrefined' (they always held that refinement was an innate quality which had little or nothing to do with 'class') but interesting, because genuine and honest. This millionaire would carefully mark his whisky bottle after each meal, to be sure that he was not cheated of any drop. He asked quaint, downright questions; 'What are your ages? I would like to know your ages,' he exclaimed a little unexpectedly one day to Mary and Jane. They laughingly satisfied his curiosity, having never entertained the smallest desire to conceal this dark secret.

On another occasion during the voyage, he asked: 'How did you Findlaters get into good society?' and Jane quickly replied, 'By grace, not by works, I assure you, Mr. Carnegie.'

[1] They had met her on the voyage out on the *Arabic*.

4

Friendships Old and New

Between Jane's last full-scale novel, *The Ladder to the Stars* in 1906 and Mary's *Tents of a Night* in 1914, momentous years had elapsed. They had borne the world to the brink of catastrophic war, on a scale which suggested to many minds the last great struggle of biblical prophesy. To the Findlaters themselves, these years had brought a number of relatively small, but for them crucial changes of circumstance and fortune.

By 1914, and well before that date, the critics had become, almost unanimously, their devoted lackeys, bowing and smiling their novels through the early stages of publication on their way to please and entertain countless readers on both sides of the Atlantic. Horizons had widened even more entrancingly since the American tour. There were yet more stimulating contacts, and more doors of interest and possibility were being thrown open invitingly. The circle of readers was ever widening and these included not only the large numbers representing popular success and a better income, but also the distinguished and discriminating, who brought the sisters fresh stimulus.

Henry James told Mary that her *Rose of Joy* had given him 'very great pleasure' (even in that comparatively straightforward remark the words were chosen with hesitation and care), and his sister-in-law, Alice James, in a letter to Jane Findlater in 1905,[1] mainly about her early books and writing, concludes, 'Do nothing else.'

Earlier in the same letter, she says,

> I want to tell you what a genius I feel you. I have re-read the *Green Graves* and we have all read *Rachel*. It is a thoroughly

[1] 4th August, 1905.

original book and so affectionately comprehending of the
temperament which for the most part is treated with derision,
or silly adoration. Many 'psychics' have passed our way and
long acquaintance has made me quick to recognize them. When
you once remarked in passing that you had made a study of the
'medium', my heart quite sank, for I said to myself, 'How *can*
she know it?' I still echo it with a different emphasis, '*How* did
she know it!' All your work and Mary's too is distinguished
and will surely speak to many a reader. I only wish that your
publishers would print another good edition of the *Green
Graves* . . .

In London, Lady Grey took Jane and Mary to the Newbolts in
Earls Terrace where they so often entertained their friends. The
'familiar faces' were those of the Beechings, the Binyons, the
Brangwyns, the Sidney Buxtons, the Calderons, the Chittys, the
Julian Corbetts, the Leonard Darwins, the Fletchers, the Eustace
Hillses, the Jack Hillses, the Bernard Hollands, the Holman
Hunts, the Cholmondeleys and a score of others. Among the
rarer guests were Sir Edward and Lady Grey, and Henry Newbolt
recalls that she 'brought the two Findlaters, Jane and Mary, and
took them away in a hansom, like a tall falconer with a bird on
either wrist'.[1]

With Henry Newbolt and his wife Margaret, the sisters made
another enduring link.

New friendships, however exhilarating, did not oust the old.
Rather were these enhanced for, like their mother, Mary and Jane
made their real friendships for life. It was therefore a cruel blow
when, early in 1906, they heard of the death of a friend so dear
and admired that no loss had been more shattering to them than,
in its very different way, that of their father in 1886.

On Sunday, 4th February, Mary writes, 'We heard of Dorothy
Grey's sudden death at Fallodon.'[2] The news was a terrible shock,
and the more so because with the return of a large measure of

[1] Sir Henry Newbolt, *My World as in my Time*, London, 1932, p. 216.
[2] Summary Diary.

health, Lady Grey had seemed in the preceding few months and weeks the very embodiment of that radiance and beauty which years of illness and semi-illness had dimmed, though never extinguished. The Findlaters had indeed scarcely known before that first glory of her youth and strength, which now seemed to be returning.

She had just been with Sir Edward in London. When they both went to dine at Windsor, she had sat beside the King,[1] who had not failed to appreciate her unusual charm and ability. She had gone north a few days in advance of her husband to prepare for his arrival, and on the morning of 1st February had set off full of energy and life in her trap, driven by the groom. In a narrow lane the horse shied violently, and she was thrown out on to her head. She never recovered consciousness and died within a few days.

In the midst of their grief, the friends who knew her best must have shared the conviction that the swiftness of her passing was what she would have desired, and sensed, however gropingly, that even the whole unanswerable tragedy was one which her noble spirit would have been too great to question.

How strange now was the recollection of a story,[2] which Mary and Jane had once been told of Lady Grey's response to a well-wisher who had desired for her a long and happy life. It was soon after her marriage with Sir Edward, and she, then radiant with happiness, had replied,

'No, not long. Only twenty years.'

Since those words were uttered in 1886, it was now just twenty years, and the story, which before had merely left with the sisters an impression of a natural inclination to avoid a dragged-out old age, instantly appeared as something like foreknowledge and burned its memory into minds as keenly alive as theirs to any suggestion of design or fulfilment in human life.

On that day of spring sunshine, with fresh sweet air such as

[1] Edward VII.

[2] Cp. Louise Creighton, *Dorothy Grey*, privately printed by Eyre and Spottiswoode & Co. Ltd., London, 1907, p. 190, where the story is also told.

Dorothy Grey had loved, the very light seemed blotted out for Mary and Jane by this unbelievable news, but their intense sorrow was soon half submerged in their deep concern for their friend Sir Edward. They wrote to him what was in their hearts and even in that darkest hour their letters seem to have brought some grains of comfort, for he replied,

> Fallodon,
> Christon Bank,
> Northumberland.
> Feb. 17. 1906.

Dear Miss Findlater,

I am very grateful for your letter and your sister's.

It is too soon for me to know yet what will become of me. I can do my work & that gains time; when the work is over I sink down and live in the past. I have had very great happiness & if I am worthy of having had it I shall live on & make something of life; but the spirit isn't in me yet: I work but I don't live.

Dorothy enjoyed your friendship & was glad that you gave it her; and I treasure what you say of her. You know enough to understand something of what it means to me to be left alone, but even I don't know it all yet, slowly every day I realize a little more; but I hope not to feel lonely for there are states of feeling when one almost gets rid of the limitation of time and can look through death.

By and bye, if both or either of you come to London, will you let me know & come to see me? I shall have a house there & shall usually be at home for luncheon. A line to the House of Commons will find me.

> Yours sincerely,
> E. Grey.

Rather more than a year later Sir Edward sent the sisters the privately printed book about Lady Grey by her friend Mrs. Creighton.[1] Again he wrote gratefully:

---

[1] Louise Creighton, *Dorothy Grey*, privately printed by Eyre and Spottiswoode and Co. Ltd., London, 1907.

Mary and Jane 'novelists of repute'

Itchen Abbas,
Alresford,
Hants.
June 7, 1907.

Dear Miss Findlater,

I could have had nothing more comforting than your letter about the book. You have found in it just what I hoped friends would find in a record of Dorothy's life. It is sad that the power of taking pleasure in common things should be so uncommon; it doesn't so much matter whether people miss this or that in the world, provided they find something & so many people find nothing, or at any rate seem to find nothing. And the world is rather a jealous world so that people don't let you enjoy things in your own way, unless you make a point of it, and if you aren't clear as to what you want you just have to drift with the crowd & lose your own shape and at the end of life no one can tell what sort of a man or woman God meant you to be.

As to giving the book to a larger public, do you think the larger public or much of it would understand? I rather shrink from giving it to many people because there is by inference so much of my own life in it. Indeed I did shrink even from having anything done for friendship only, but the hope that it would be helpful just in the way you have found it overcame that; and now I am very glad because it is so well done & preserves a record of personality, much of which must have been lost otherwise.

There isn't much to tell about myself – the work[1] is enormous: it hasn't left time to read either *The Ladder to the Stars* or *The Blind Bird's Nest,* though I noted both as they came out. But I like your saying that one's life is not in the work; that is true more than ever & the question at the end of life should be not 'What have you done?' but 'What are you?'

Yours very sincerely,
Edward Grey.

[1] G. M. Trevelyan, *Lord Grey of Fallodon,* London, 1937. Grey was Foreign Minister from December 1905 to December 1916.

The design which Mary always sought in the lives of individuals is evident in almost every turn of her own, as if by her very expectancy she attracted to herself coherence and compensation. Immediately preceding the entry of their great loss on 4th February in the death of Dorothy Grey, she writes (they were living at Mount Stuart, Torquay, at this time) for 3rd February, 1906.

At Mrs. Bridgmans' we met Diana Cholmondeley and our long friendship with the Cholmondeleys began.

As this friendship grew, it was rather with Mary Cholmondeley and yet more with her sister Victoria that the intimacy was closest. These developments, however, lay in the future, for although the Findlaters met Mary Cholmondeley in the following April, they did not see Victoria until a year later, in Venice.

On the same page of the Diary, Mary writes under February 6th, 'We first made acquaintance with Lady Crawford and Jane and Mabel Lindsay.'[1] This also was to be a friendship for life. It was indeed as if these particular bright stars had risen above the Findlaters' horizon as one of the most brilliant in their sky vanished from mortal sight.

In March 1906 'Chattie' Stewart and her mother came to stay in Torquay, and Mary writes; 'We saw the Stewarts every day and the Lindsays constantly.'

In May, the two sisters took rooms in Lower Grosvenor Place for a few weeks, and there 'we saw a number of people, M. Cholmondeley, May Sinclair, Kate Riggs and many others'.

Thus between visits to and from friends both old and new, sojourns in London and summer tours in Scotland which included Edinburgh, Cockenzie House, Ardvorlich and Wick, the months passed. There was also now considerable correspondence with friends in America, who had entered the inner circle and with whom Mary and Jane shared joys, griefs, ideas and confidences.

In June 1906 Alice James wrote:

[1] Margaret, Dowager Countess of Crawford, was widow of the eighth Earl of Crawford and Balcarres. Lady Mabel was the fifth and Lady Jane the seventh and youngest child of this marriage.

95 Irving St. Cambe.
June 5, 1906.

Dear Mary,

Day after day I have meant to write you of our strange works
and ways and daily I have instead answered the trivial note or
heeded the present interruption instead . . . But long ere this
you and Jane will have perceived that my *tempo* is a slow one. I
hope that you also understand that in time I shall always be
heard from at least by you two dear girls whose coming was
such a delight to me. You would laugh if you knew how entirely you seemed to belong to me.

I am more sorry than I can say to hear that your mother's
eyes are failing, and then you have had the great loss of your
friend.[1] She must have been an exquisite creature. The departure of such as she, so needed in this world, seems to speak of
another existence beside whose superior claims our poor life
is not to be counted. How does Sir Edward Grey live without
her? After her companionship other people must seem to him
as shadows.

After an industrious winter of writing the novel which had
been begun years before as *Pitmilly* and was to be completed as
Crossriggs, a winter which was enlivened by visits from old friends
and the companionship of the Lindsays, Mary and Jane set off
in April with Charlotte Stewart and her mother, for their first
visit to Italy. They went via Paris and Lausanne, where they had
a glimpse of their friend Mrs. Roberton. In Venice there were
other friends, but of these, the bright particular star was Victoria
Cholmondeley, whom they saw for the first time there. Beyond
their great pleasure in getting to know her, their astonished delight in the beauty of Venice and the recounting of one or two
minor incidents of comedy, discomfort or both, Mary never had
much to say about this sojourn in Italy, except that the life of the
English in and around Venice was 'too artificial' for her and
Jane.

[1] Dorothy Grey.

Victoria Cholmondeley came to stay with the Findlaters at Torquay in the following September. Like her sister, Mary Cholmondeley she was delightful company, though in a rather different way. The Findlaters used to say that both sisters took great pleasure in this world, but that it was not their only pleasure. In a very special degree was this true of Victoria, for she possessed a shining serenity and a quick unusual extra sense able to pierce beyond the material. Mary and Jane were told by a former neighbour and old friend of the Cholmondeleys, Mr. Rowland Corbet,[1] that in her girlhood Victoria had changed after an illness. Before it she was still a sweet child, but when she recovered she had come to a maturity of spirit and of perception which was something more than maturity of age. The Scottish family doctor used to fulminate against what he felt to be the wastage of Victoria's life in nursing first her old father, then later her sister Mary, and always in smoothing the difficulties of her other sister, Diana. Yet even when physical and nervous strain took their toll, Mary and Jane felt that nothing ever dimmed the radiance of her spirit.

The Findlaters' happy summer was followed by a sad winter. December 1907 brought illness to the Mount Stuart household, especially to Mora and her mother. Margaret Roberton came down from Scotland to help the stricken family, but on Christmas Eve Mrs. Findlater's condition suddenly worsened and on Christmas Day at noon she died.

In one of her books,[2] Jane observes that the four walls of a house, the chairs and tables even, have the power of bringing back the past too vividly, and whereas the poor must quietly resume life again in the little room of poignant memories, haunted by the illness they have nursed, the rich can generally leave the scene of their troubles behind, which is the next best thing to leaving the troubles themselves behind. The Findlaters were not rich, but they were not now obliged to count every penny they spent, and they thankfully accepted Mary Cholmondeley's invitation to come to stay with her in Knightsbridge. It was late in that cold January

[1] The Rev. Rowland Corbet, author of *Letters of a Mystic of the Present Day.*
[2] *The Story of a Mother,* p. 246.

when they arrived at Albert Gate Mansions. Hardly could the Cholmondeleys have found a dwelling more at variance with everything characteristic of themselves, but once out of the noisy traffic-filled street, past the door on the upper floor with its tinted glass, suggestive of Tottenham Court Road, the atmosphere changed. Colours were subdued, harmonious, ingratiatingly faded, furniture was worn but elegant, a picture, a bit of old china, would be always perfectly placed.

The unerring taste, the touch which put the rare, the pleasing object in exactly the right position, were old Mr. Cholmondeley's. When the Findlaters paid their first visit, he was still a sort of presiding genius in the house, reclining on couch or arm-chair at the fireside, graciously welcoming or dismissing the guests, usually now utterly vague as to who they were. His strangely high voice among the low, subdued tones of his daughters', sounded like a perpetual obligato accompaniment to all the movement and life of the household.

There were frequent parties, prepared with great care, but with all the art that conceals art. Mary Cholmondeley liked to have the room prepared with one large, heavy, apparently immovable arm-chair as an anchor or pivot, with lighter chairs grouped around it. Diana poured out, Victoria moved about among the guests. Mary herself was chief hostess and the life of any party, for she was excellent company. She liked her guests well mixed, with an interesting variety. The intellectual level had to be assured, but she would, if possible, as she explained, 'have a sprinkling of Duchesses, to add, tone, not of the weightier kind'. Finally there were still the representatives of the young men who half a decade earlier used to inquire of one another, 'Have you read *Pottage*?'[1]

The friendship between the Findlaters and the Cholmondeleys grew and flourished. There would have been congenial soil for this in the background of both families, which had a number of essentials in common, although there were many contrasts

[1] *Red Pottage*, published in 1899, which caused a considerable stir and made Mary Cholmondeley's fame. She had already published four novels, the first of which, *The Danvers Jewels*, had appeared in 1887.

provided by Rectory and Manse, Shropshire and Perthshire alone. To Mary and Jane the Cholmondeleys were distinctively and profoundly English. In fact, this Englishness was characteristically composed with an admixture of Norman French and Welsh ancestors. The strain of hymn writing in the Cholmondeley connection was to be found in no less a person than Bishop Heber, their father's uncle.[1] The breeding of the Cholmondeleys was aristocratic, they were indigenous and of the county. Hodnet Rectory, the home of their childhood, had been more like a spacious country house than a parsonage. There were entertainments, parties, dances, but living was not soft or very comfortable. Winter cold was severe and, like the Brontës, the sisters would pace up and down the schoolroom to warm themselves.

At Hodnet Rectory, there was a cheering element of gaiety and festivity and a considerable amount of company, which the Scottish counterpart lacked. The Lochearnhead Manse was much poorer, much smaller and more restricting, but in both homes there was culture and Christian liberality of mind. Sectarianism in its cruder form could not exist in the presence of Mr. Cholmondeley or Mr. Findlater. Gaiety was stronger in the one, intellectual capacity in the other. Mr. Cholmondeley's generous convictions were in his blood, part of his being and behaviour and of his heritage as an English gentleman. He never questioned them as did his children, but his daughters started from a basis of sweetness and light provided by his attitude, which gave them a direction which they never lost. Mr. and Mrs. Findlater eventually decided, after careful thought, that they could not believe in everlasting punishment. Mr. Cholmondeley felt that he could not do without 'the devil', but the comradeship of fellow Christians was more important to all of them than any dogmas or doctrines. They were not interested in barring out other denominations from their churches or from any part of their services. They were entirely lacking in the arrogance which sees itself as 'set apart'. Other Christians were fellow soldiers, whether of different regiments or not.

[1] Mary Cholmondeley: *Under One Roof*, a Family Record, London, 1918, p. 10.

There were ways in which, to their children, these parents seemed old-fashioned or narrow, but they handed on the essentials of the Christian faith and lived their beliefs in a way so absolutely sincere that it could not fail to impress the minds of the next generation. From such pastures it was natural that the young people, looking for wider and richer sustenance, should, as did many serious girls of their day, turn to the works of Emerson. In his nobility and breadth of outlook, his magnificent phrases and warm eloquence, in the fervour of his exhortation, balanced always by cool sanity, they found what they needed. There was nothing too luxuriant or overheated in his meditations. A Northerner and a Protestant, the atmosphere of his inspiration was for them like the bright, invigorating autumnal weather to which critics became fond of comparing the atmosphere of the Findlaters' books. No wonder that Mary Findlater and Mary Cholmondeley[1] both became disciples of Ralph Waldo Emerson, and that this influence made an imprint upon the minds of both which was never lost.

It was during the same visit to London that the Findlaters went for the first time to see Lady Tennant at Queen Anne's Gate, and, as Mary expressed it, 'our friendship with Pamela Glenconner[2] began'.

Through their old friend Charles Gray (who was her doctor) they came to know, at this time, Paula Schuster, of the well-known merchant and banking family, of Frankfurt. Her mother's father was Hofrath Pfeiffer who founded the Hofbank at Stuttgart, a strikingly handsome man whose portrait shows a face distinguished by intellectual refinement. On both sides of the family there was Rabbi ancestry as well as great business ability. Nor were statesmanship and leadership lacking.[3] The family, which had long possessed trading interests with England, migrated

[1] Mary Cholmondeley belonged to the same generation as the Findlaters, though she was slightly senior to them, born at Hodnet in Shropshire on June 8th, 1859, third child and eldest daughter of the Rev. Richard Hugh Cholmondeley, died in London on 15th July, 1925.

[2] She afterwards became Lord Grey's second wife.

[3] Paula Jones, *Memories of Marie Schuster*, London, 1949.

to this country in 1869 so that Paula, the only daughter and youngest child, born in 1865, was brought up mainly in England.

The Schusters,[1] Reisses[2] and Pfeiffers were Jews who combined 'a Puritan devotion' to religion and duty with the 'keenest appreciation of beauty in nature, art, music and literature'.[3] Their Judaism, especially that of the Pfeiffers, seemed deeply coloured by the ideals of Christianity, so that it was a comparatively easy step for the family, in the generation of Paula's parents, to become Christian.

All their gifts, artistic, intellectual, commercial, their philanthropy, their lofty and strict ideals were characteristic of the finest flower of that German Jew type which they represented. Paula's education was carried on at university level, and of her three brothers, the second, Arthur, became a distinguished physicist.

Paula was wealthy, a friend and patroness of artists, intellectuals and especially those whose religion or philosophy was blended with mysticism. Dean Inge, the Rowland Corbets, Walter de la Mare, the Cholmondeleys of course, the Newbolts and many others were in her circle. Jane and Mary were attracted by qualities so unexpectedly mingled as those which went to the making of this Jewess, for she was both worldly and other-worldly wise, shrewd and generous, philanthropic in most practical, and yet far from wholly material, ways. She was absorbed in good works, usually unmindful of her appearance yet capable of the splendour of an Eastern Princess. The Findlaters, who particularly disliked ostentatious jewellery or dressing, agreed that Paula had the oriental gift of looking better with every ornament she put on. Hung round with chains and gems, garbed in orange velvet, she seemed like a veritable Queen of Sheba. The wide

[1] The name Schuster was said to be derived from that of the Persian town Suza, which in German was Schuster, and it was supposed that the family had originally been Persian Jews.

[2] Reisses were, along with the Schusters, among the leading Jewish families in Frankfurt. v. Paula Jones, op. cit., p. 11.

[3] ibid, p. 10.

ranging tastes and preoccupations of the Schusters[1] always fascinated Mary's imagination and she relished the fact that one of Paula's relatives spent absorbing leisure hours in watching the pulsations in the leg of a fly.

Paula Schuster understood well the stresses and strains in the lives of those less fortunate than herself, and she had the capacity to give without hurting or embarrassing the recipient. Mary and Jane occasionally accepted gifts from her, which they could never have brought themselves to take from other people. She invited Walter de la Mare to pay a long visit (before he was famous) so that he might have an appendix operation (the prospect of which appalled him) in the cheerful surroundings and comfort of home, and there be tended with the utmost care.

When the Findlaters first met De la Mare at their friend's house, Mary was specially struck by the strangeness of his eyes. 'Quite unlike ordinary human eyes (she would say), but resembling those of some beautiful wild creature.' She had seen none comparable then, she used to declare, until, years later, she met a relative of her own, a retired officer, and of him she remarked 'A man with eyes like that should never have been in the army as a profession.'

Thus it was that she and Jane would scrutinize those they met and build up 'a person' from external items, physical or sartorial, sometimes to the ordinary onlooker infinitesimal, but for them full of significance. Was this meticulous observation something that they had learnt from their admired friend, Dr. Joseph Bell?

They always wanted people to be their own peculiar selves, to preserve their special idiosyncrasy. The result might be more or very much less to the liking of Mary and Jane, but the genuineness counted for much. Authoritarianism in religion, thought or politics was to them the deadly foe. There was nothing tepid, vague or shapeless about the liberty of the mind, the vital integrity which they valued so highly. Their ideal was in a sense old-fashioned. It was to be sought and defended by reason, but it was nothing static or stereotyped. It was alive, and their search for

[1] Her brother was Sir Felix, the 1st Baronet, created 1906, and another brother was a very distinguished Physicist, Professor Arthur Schuster.

truth was a driving force with a definite direction, a quest of infinite and varied preoccupation. For them anything and everything under the sun could be rationally considered and spiritually enhanced. Above all a human being was the most lovable and fascinating complex in all creation.

Mary took naturally to the Platonic idea that love, human love, was the beginning of wisdom, the shadow of 'heavenly love' – towards which it was the first step in the ladder. Essential for her, she maintained, in grasping at all greater and higher significance, was the perfect understanding and harmony that existed between herself and Jane. From that her comprehension of the spiritual began, from that stemmed belief, hope and all the little (she made no great claims for it) comprehension that she had.

The prospect was brightening and broadening again. The shadows of loss and death were receding into happier memories of life and love and friendship which suffused present and future as well as past. Southfield Mount was now once more the Findlaters' home.[1] The far more congenial surroundings and society of Paignton were a pleasant exchange for those of Torquay, which had always seemed to Mary and Jane stuffy and enervating, physically, mentally and spiritually. *Crossriggs* was published. The reviewers chorused approval and appreciation. The public bought it delightedly.

The sisters were often away, staying with friends in London, or elsewhere in the south, and yearly visits to Scotland continued during the summer months. There they would roam from the Cadells of Cockenzie to the Robertons up in Wick, seeing many other friends *en route* and returning to old haunts, including Lochearnhead, where on one occasion they had to clear up the Borthwick Aunts' former house. Confronted with the formidable volumes of Aunt Jane's Journal, Mary and Jane, exhausted and desperate, put them on a boat, rowed out on Loch Earn, 'and dropped them into its deepest waters'.

This was half regretted by the sisters afterwards, but Mary maintained that, despite interesting entries, the diary was too

[1] In September 1908, they were able to buy it.

overwhelmingly full of a 'rather moony piety'. She and Jane must have relented to the extent of retaining a volume or two, for later she alludes to 'reading an odd volume of our good Aunt Jane's *Journals*.' These, Mary confessed, moved her 'greatly to laughter at times' especially in their overpowering absurdity when 'describing our own youth', but time had brought more sympathetic insight, for she also declares, 'Somehow the goodness of our Elders, in spite of all their timidities and small weaknesses of character, seems more and more apparent as we get farther away from them.'[1]

The two often stayed at Netherhampton, a beautiful old house which the Newbolts had gone to share with Henry Furse in 1907. It stood on the edge of the Wiltshire Downs and its history went back to the early years of Elizabeth I. There were later associations with Harriet Grove, Shelley's cousin and first love.

Mary and Jane used to feel how deeply mellowed with culture and warmed by civilization these great houses of the south were in contrast to the ruder, bleaker dwellings of the north. Yet, although surroundings meant much, people always meant far more. It was the inhabitants of a house who mattered supremely, and Mary wrote later[2] of the Newbolts, with whom she had managed to arrange a meeting in London,

> I snatched one delightful dinner with the Newbolts and Shaw Stewarts. Margaret Newbolt looking like a fair October morning with her peculiar delicious freshness and remoteness from the rough and tumble of life: partly the result of her deafness which gives her a kind of aloofness from the crowd. That freshness which reminds one of woods and dew is a quality so rare in middle age that it strikes surprise. 'Sir Henry' was pinched and overstrained looking but is always interesting.

There were visits now to the Cholmondeleys in Suffolk, for at Ufford Victoria and Mary had found a summer retreat for themselves on the edge of a friend's estate.[3] Mary and Jane savoured

[1] Letter to Marion Cadell, 25th April, 1916.
[2] Letter to Marion Cadell, 12th November, 1915.
[3] The first visit is recorded in the Summary Diary, 22nd May, 1909.

the appropriate Englishness of the setting which their friends had found for themselves. Down a sequestered lane they came to the little house. From it there was a glimpse of the grey village church and a roof or two. Beyond the house lay king-cup meadows, and poplars brushed the white clouds that sailed along those great pacific skies above it. In the garden the sisters strolled with Mary and Victoria and perhaps some fellow guest, carefully chosen with that ever unobtrusive art which made the perfect success of the Cholmondeley's London parties.

In October 1908, the William Jameses came to Paignton. Mrs. James and her daughter Peggy stayed with the Findlaters at Southfield Mount, and William James at the Redcliffe Hotel. Perfectly congenial company and fascinating talk, where question and speculation were enlarged and enriched by William's far-sighted mind, made this a particularly happy time. Two years later and too soon, William James died, and the struggle out of overwhelming grief, back to everyday life, as she knew he would have wished her to live it, is reflected in the letters of Alice James to the Findlaters in the following months and years. To Mary she wrote,

> You divined how entire the life of the family centred in William and how strangely lifeless the house is without him.[1]

and to Jane,

> I have had to live just day by day, trying to do the best I could for the children and for Henry, who was ill-fitted to bear shock of William's going. You see, we thought if we could get him home, the children and the quiet of Cambridge would cheer and rest him. But he wanted to go and made no tarrying. He said to me 'Rejoice when I go' and I want to be glad for him, but it is not yet well enough with me for that.

Later she adds, 'The children are all four at home and Henry is spending the winter with us. We keep cheerful and help one another as you help me with your kind feeling for us.'[2]

[1] Thanksgiving Evening, 24th November, 1910.
[2] Letter from 95 Irving Street, Cambridge, 24th November, 1910.

The process of recovery was slow. Early in 1914, apologizing for a long silence, Alice James writes to Jane,

... just when I should be more responsive than ever before to the friends that are left to me, then with the strange incalculableness of sorrow I grow dumb. It is an unworthy way, and after this I am going to be alive again. And one of its symptoms is that I feel as if I should see you and Mary again. You are so easy to talk to, and so *adorable* to listen to! I am hoping that you will let your house and then make me a long visit. And this time there will be no journey into the wilderness. If ever you do wish me to advertise your house for you, I shall gladly do so. Expenses do increase alarmingly, and there comes a time when simplification is one's deepest demand, and *freedom*. As you say to stop thinking about ordinary legitimate expenses.

This, Alice James explains, has come to her since her sons finished their long education, and she goes on to tell of her daughter Peggy's hope of seeing Mary and Jane when she joins a friend in 'a little flat near her Uncle in Cheyne Walk' where she intends to spend 'the next ten weeks'.

With Henry James the sisters became further acquainted, meeting him often at the houses of mutual friends, corresponding on various topics[1] and exchanging visits. It was a friendship they appreciated and enjoyed, although it lacked the complete ease and felicity of their relationship with the William Jameses.

At a small party arranged by Agnes and Alice Kemp for Henry James, conversation was flowing happily and the chief guest in excellent vein, when the front door bell rang. It sounded like a knell. 'How awful,' murmured Agnes Kemp to Jane, 'if it should be the wrong person!' They all knew full well that an aggressive intruder might put off Henry James completely and ruin the party. But as they waited with some apprehension, endeavouring to patch up the talk, in walked Richard Burdon Haldane.

---

[1] So far as I know, only three of his letters to Jane and Mary Findlater were preserved.

Conversation soon mounted on wings. The two men got on perfectly. No party could have been more successful.

There were often amusing little episodes of mutual impatience, when Henry James hesitated for a word and Mary, eager to hear what he had to say, quickly supplied him with half a dozen or more. But he would brush aside her suggestions until he had found one that hit the mark exactly. Had he met Mrs. So-and-so in America? Yes, he had met her and her . . . This admission was followed by a long pause. 'Her . . .' he waited, searching for the word. Mary suggested several alternatives, which were cast away with protesting, quick gestures, until James slowly rolled out 'and her *monstrous* progeny!'

At one time, the Findlaters carried on a monumental correspondence for a week or more about a visit that he was planning to pay them. Finally the edifice of letters collapsed and the plan disintegrated, presumably from sheer exhaustion on both sides. Their most uncomfortable encounter was the occasion on which Henry James invited the sisters to lunch with him.

My dear Findlaters (he wrote),

This is fine about your lunching Saturday & I shall rejoice to see you. But can you stay your proud stomachs to 1.45 sharp? Then I shall count upon you.

James added a postscript,

I shall be quite alone. Also I find it's more than kind of you to have written about Polmont.[1]

Duly, upon Saturday, at 1.45 sharp, the ladies stood upon the doorstep of 21 Carlyle Mansions, Cheyne Walk, S.W., only to find that they were not expected and had come on the 'wrong day'. In vain they tried to withdraw tactfully and lunch elsewhere. The apologetic and agitated host would not hear of this. He had lunched already, but insisted on having another meal prepared and set before his guests. None of the party enjoyed themselves one whit. When the sisters got home and looked at their invitation, they found that the mistake was not theirs but his.

[1] Letter of 24th January, 1914.

The postscript of James's letter referred to the Findlaters' efforts to discover anything possible about an ancestor of Henry James who lived at Polmont near Stirling. This was the James's maternal great-grandfather on the mother's side, 'that is our mother's mother's father', as Henry James explains in *A Small Boy and Others*.[1] The Findlaters' researches led them to suppose that Robertson must have been some sort of small shopkeeper in Polmont and he had evidently 'sat under' their great grandfather,[2] Mr. William Finlay, who was Minister of Polmont.

> You are very interesting (so wrote Henry James to the Findlaters) about our Polmont coincidence, & we must have all talk of it. I shall then ask you if there is anyone you know in the place who could copy the inscription on a memorial of some sort (presumably a mere slab or tablet) which I *believe* to have been placed there to my great grandfather & naming certain bounties which he had rendered the place after he had settled in New York. It may have yielded to time, or I may have been mistaken, & that's what I want to clear up (& other things of other sorts) together, & I am yours both most truly,
>
> Henry James.[3]

The discussions and inquiries went on and were carried further by Alice James, after her brother-in-law's death, in collaboration with the Findlaters. Before this, however, Mary had reached her own conclusion, which was that 'Henrry', as she called him with her peculiar continental rolling of the R, did not really much care for this particular ancestor, 'who belonged to a rrather (for him) unattrractive social strratum.'

Throughout the pre-war period, the Findlaters' output of novels had continued. Three years separated their second book written together, from the first. *Penny Monypenny* was finished early in 1911 and published later in that year Like *Crossriggs*, it belonged

[1] Op. cit. London, 1913, p. 7.

[2] The maternal grandfather of Sarah Borthwick, who became the Rev. Eric Findlater's wife and mother of the authoresses Mary and Jane.

[3] Letter of 21st January, 1914, from 21 Carlyle Mansions, Cheyne Walk, S.W.

essentially to an age which was still intact and undisrupted. There had been fears and scares about German aggression, but the talk of their liberal friends, the Greys, Haldanes, Lady Frances Balfour and others, had not left immediate apprehension in the sisters' minds. When in May 1914 they had returned from a week with the Cholmondeleys at Ufford, Violet Jacob[1] came for a brief stay with the Findlaters, and Mary notes: 'She anticipated the war, & told us so, but we did not believe her'.

[1] Violet Jacob, poetess and novelist 1863–1946. Born at Montrose. Her maiden name was Kennedy-Erskine. She married Major Otway Jacobs of the Hussars and spent some years in India. Her novels included *The Sheep Stealers*, 1902; *The Interloper*, 1904; *The History of Aythan Waring*, 1908. She published many volumes of poems some of which were in the Angus dialect.

5

1914–1923

After the publication of *Penny Monypenny* in 1912, it was many a long year before Mary and Jane collaborated in another novel. Numbers of Jane's short stories, specially her gipsy stories, were yet to appear and the sisters combined in an amusing little account of 'doing for themselves' (Mary, in particular was not domestically minded or gifted) in war time, which they called *Content with Flies*. Had it not been for the 1914–18 war, they would almost certainly have produced another full-scale novel after two years or so, but like many of their compatriots, even the more elderly, they had their 'war work' and this absorbed much time and energy.

By July the Findlaters had begun to have second thoughts about Violet Jacob's fears. Visitors were coming and going, 'Pamela Glenconner and little Stephen', then their old friends, the Macgillivrays, but now thoughts and conversation were dominated by the increasing political tension.

A few days after the declaration of war on 4th August, the sisters began to work in the local hospital at Paignton, 'cleaning sinks, etc.' which Mary found 'very futile and exhausting'. Certainly their gifts were put to better use when they took on the hospital library. They appealed to their friends, authors or otherwise, and met with a good response. Rudyard Kipling wrote encouragingly from Burwash, reminiscing about their meeting years previously at Dunrobin, and sending off immediately a box of books. Cunard & Company offered them six hundred volumes, to be selected by themselves.

Mora had volunteered for nursing and went to take up her duties at Newton Stewart. Down in Paignton, Mary and Jane soon began to feel the impact of the appalling losses in men at the front and of the mourning all around them. Their thoughts and emotions, their intense concern for and interest in the wounded men in hospital are reflected in Mary's letters to Marion Cadell at this time. 'I wonder,' she asks, 'if the Colonel[1] visits the wounded much? If it were not for his deafness I'm sure he would do them no end of good. Did I tell you how Henry James has simply renewed his youth by this? "Have your men anyone to visit them?" he asked. "I do not mean to *see* them merely – of course I know that – but have they anyone of *intelligence* (he puts such awful meaning into the word and pauses on it) to hear their stories?'

Mary used to recall how James said that when he entered a ward, he would let his glance travel along the beds until he saw among the occupants a face that had a real gleam of intelligence. To that bedside he would go and begin a conversation. He was delighted with the success of his method.

The Findlater household soon began to feel the rise in the cost of living. The sisters tried to laugh at the minor horrors of wartime, such as depressing females, more than usually direful, because of anxiety and 'war-hats'. The point where absurdity and tragedy met always touched a sensitive nerve in Mary. '*Is* it Spring?' Mary asks sadly, in a letter to Marion Cadell. 'I can hardly believe it. No one takes any notice this year tho' the first primroses have begun & the long whistles of thrushes in the February evenings.'

Yet there was one person who, in her own way, was taking great account of the oncoming spring. Bunder, the Findlaters' faithful maid from Cockenzie with her ally 'the char', in a campaign of cleaning was 'slashing about with pails of soapy water',[2] and making the landings impassable with chairs and tables dragged forth from their usual sphere of impassive usefulness to be cleaned, where they obtruded their legs and bulk to the discomfort of those who were (it is true) ultimately to benefit, but to the immediate joy of no one except those actively engaged.

[1] Marion Cadell's father

[2] Letter to Marion Cadell from Southfield Mount, Paignton, 11th February, 1915.

Bunder had, in fact, been in her element since the outbreak of war. At the hospital, as a visitor, no quarrels could ever deter her and she was even more of a success than Henry James, for she commanded assets on a level where he could not compete. She would carry to her wounded fellow-countrymen iced cakes 'covered with flags and surrounded with sumptuous garlands of red, white and blue . . .' together with tins of shortbread which she had baked, stamping each biscuit with a vigorous Scotch thistle.

Mary and Jane felt the need to escape for a while from the little turmoil and the restrictions of life in Paignton. London was a change from all this, but brought small consolation, although meeting the friends of their wider acquaintance once more, was stimulating. Late one night, returning about eleven o'clock from a dinner and long evening's talk with Paula Schuster, Mary and Jane arrived at the door of 6 Glebe Place, Chelsea, where they were staying, to see a group of people collected on the steps. Then,

a huge dishevelled figure rose from her seat on the top step, and advanced to greet us with outstretched arms, calling so that the whole road could hear, 'I've been sitting on your doorstep for three quarters of an hour, & you wouldn't come in!' At first I was bewildered – then saw it was poor dear Ellen Terry. Alas! for Youth & Beauty! Paint is hard enough on a young face but an aged, seamed, harrowed one, covered with powder and with reddened mouth is unspeakably ghastly. She was supported by a little wilted daughter-in-law & as she embraced us her hat blew off & whirled down nearly to the Cottage at the end & she stood with her dishevelled grey hair & her painted mouth laughing at her Cabman's efforts to retrieve it. Such a figure of unconscious tragedy.

In a few minutes the driver had returned, breathless but triumphant, bearing the errant hat. As he handed it to the owner, a great actress's power suddenly asserted itself, outshining all the sordid details and absurdity of the situation. She turned towards the man with a queenly movement and such an exquisitely gracious 'Thank you, Mr. Cabby', that he went off (so Mary often told me in describing the scene) as if he walked on air.

The sisters brought their visitor in. Everyone else in the house had gone to bed, so they sat talking together 'in the low parlour' until midnight. 'Charming company still, even tho' she can hardly remember her own name,' concluded Mary.[1] She and Jane always felt that Ellen Terry was as delightful and remarkable off the stage as on it, and in this was unlike some great actors whose presence shrinks when they are not behind the footlights.[2]

Apart from seeing their friends, this sojourn in London was much occupied with preparations for their great experiment. So-called civilized life was never going to be the same again. The servantless age, which so many years ago their Uncle Mac had foretold, was almost with them. Other women, even less fitted for it than themselves, might be driven into a corner of despair by unrelenting circumstances. What could be done to help them shoulder the burden courageously, competently and, to this end, lightheartedly?

The writers foresaw that the 'flower of civilized life' might fade among people of moderate income and an existence much less elegant take its place. Yet, as Mary and Jane showed in their account of this venture, the bleak prospect was not, or need not be, so bleak as it looked. It might indeed be rather exciting, even exhilarating, and certainly amusing if one was prepared to laugh at oneself. When the experiment at Kincardine Cottage, Aviemore was over the sisters felt that something had been permanently gained, although within a few hours of arriving at the Central Manse, Wick, to stay with their old friends the Robertons, the chains of habit were upon them once more. 'We lie in bed and have our hot water brought as usual. We sit and eat meals cooked and served by others and already the cottage life seems almost a

[1] Letter to Marion Cadell, 28th May, 1915.

[2] Cf. Bernard Shaw, *Ellen Terry and Bernard Shaw, a Correspondence,* ed. Christopher St. John, London, 1931, Preface, p. xx.

dream.'[1] But the sisters went back to Devon to write about it and to prepare a collection of short stories[2] throughout that winter. In February 1916 came the cheerful news of the engagement of their friend Paula Schuster to Sir Lawrence Jones. There were friends in Torquay, the Kemps and William Macgregor, whose society they greatly enjoyed. But influenza was rife and all the time there was a sense of tension, as Mary wrote to Marion Cadell.

The feeling that one was 'holding one's breath' in wondering 'how this awful struggle is going on in France' and she continues:

> The two subjects of private interest to us have been, of course, Paula Schuster's marriage and the death of dear Henry James. It is as if a light had gone out for everyone who knew him. The force & depth of the man's personality, & the sense he gave you of having drunk so deeply of experience as to have got almost more out of life than is given to ordinary mortals, made him a friend whose like we shall never see again. I grudge that we knew him only for ten years . . .

> His sister-in-law (Mrs. William James) and his dear niece Peggy & young Henry were all with him for several weeks towards the end. Last week Alice wrote that she had no nursing to do, but he liked her to sit with him most of the time. Now we are going to try to get her to come down to us for a little when her last duties there are over. I wonder what will happen to his charming old house at Rye?[3]

To this invitation Alice James replied on 22nd March, from 21 Carlyle Mansions, Cheyne Walk, S.W.

My dear Mary,

You will understand how I have come to leave the letters I cared for most, to be answered last. It was easier to answer

[1] Letter to Marion Cadell 18th August, 1915.

[2] *Seen and Heard Before and After* 1914.

[3] Letter to Marion Cadell, 1st March, 1916.

the more remote expressions of sympathy, though this adjective is undeserved for all the letters have been full of real feeling. Your quotation from the *Spectator* of February 19th is most beautiful and it so describes Henry and our feeling about him. Through all the physical disarray and mental bewilderment his great spirit was erect and uninvaded, so patient of the detaining body and revealing itself in many ways. Peggy said, 'No one could have watched him and had a doubt of immortality.' So it seems well with him and I rejoice for him. For ourselves the loss is immense but when I look on this sorrowing world I feel ashamed to speak of it.

I want to come to you for a little, and as soon as we know something more about our affairs I shall write and ask if our dates can suit yours. We have to let and dismantle this flat and settle Lamb House before we go home in July.

With much love to you and Jane,

Ever yours affectionately,
Alice H. James.

Mary had been reading Bergson and finding release from notions which may well have tended to harden over much in the flame of that Calvinism in which she and Jane were brought up:

Lately I've been contented with the thought (suggested by reading Bergson) that *there isn't any future* – that is in the sense of there being no great sort of map of our future in the hands of the Creator – as we used to be taught, but that life being continuous Creation – Being – every moment unfolds something utterly new and unknown. We make it as we go by right and efficient action, & it cannot be foreseen. Somehow that is more comforting than to think we are just slowly moving on to perhaps some dark event – set at a fixed moment & all prepared beforehand. I've expressed it very badly, but perhaps you will see what I mean.[1]

Into the routine of proof-correcting, and writing against the

[1] Letter to Marion Cadell, 19th April, 1916.

background of spring cleaning, during those cold, bright April days, came

> a long letter from Paula . . . her first as 'Lady Jones' – so happy, so natural that it makes one's heart glad. 'Sir Lawrence' now thinks (no wonder!) that her wardrobe requires a little renewal in spite of War Economy, & she begs us to come & stay with them in the end of May, & give her some hints in regard to it. She wants us to know him & wants 'nothing to be changed' about her friends. That dear woman is impossible, as Sir Lawrence himself makes a good solid change to start with, but I'm glad she feels securely happy.[1]

Accordingly, in a few weeks' time, towards the end of May, Mary and Jane went up to London and paid their first visit to Paula Jones at Harrington Gardens after her marriage, enjoyed her interesting and unusual company, met and liked Sir Lawrence, quickly realizing the kindness that lay beneath his amusingly blunt remarks and ways, and the fundamental harmony that existed between two personalities, despite differences of background and tradition, which might have produced nothing but clashing discord.

That summer, Mary and Jane said good-bye to Alice James at the Chelsea flat for the last time[2] and almost within the year they had bidden farewell to Charlotte Stewart, which was a sadder parting because they knew it was the last. The intervening winter had been spent in desultory war work at Paignton and in helping to settle Agnes and Alice Kemp into their new home. Now the Findlaters decided to undertake some more systematic war work and in August 1917 settled at Glebe Place, almost immediately paying their first visit to the Hospital at Denmark Hill with Lady Brassey. Early in September they began their work in the library at Camberwell. They went there six days a week through air raids and fogs, and as the war months slowly passed, often with great weariness, but they were keenly interested in their work and

[1] Letter to Marion Cadell, 25th April, 1916.
[2] Summary Diary, 3rd August, 1916.

found it very rewarding. Routine was relieved from time to time by seeing friends. Lady Henry Somerset, for instance, with whom they lunched, 'at her delicious old rooms in Gray's Inn' at a table of scrubbed oak with Breton pottery and heard about her work at Duxhurst for workhouse babies and unmarried mothers. Or they would spend the day with the Glenconners, going on perhaps with Pamela Glenconner and Sir Edward Grey to a concert at Mrs. Gordon Woodhouse's.

The friendship between the Findlaters and Lady Glenconner had grown and ripened. There was a literary bond, and for the sisters the attraction of a temperament both genial and sweet, highly sensitive to the life of young things and of childhood. When she loved, Pamela Glenconner was capable of coaxing back to life the 'bruised reed' or of kindling the 'smoking flax'. Her muse was a slight affair, as she herself expressed it, in Robert Herrick's words, 'my small pipe best fits my little note'.[1] Yet, the 'small pipe', if seldom very original, had the charm, at times, of a robin's song, especially when it touched some note of the ancient countryside, traditional verse, or balladry. Above all, Pamela Glenconner adored (that abused word is here appropriate) her children. For her they embodied all that the poets had claimed for childhood of insight, other wordly wisdom and celestial radiance. They taught her, so she firmly believed, far more than she could teach them, although, in her view, this did not imply perfection or lack of need for careful training.

Lady Glenconner was still, at this date, a beautiful woman. Both the Findlaters felt drawn to her, but Mary in her absolute sincerity, found herself unable always to enter into what she called 'the child mystique' of their friend. Jane's natural sympathies carried her further than Mary in this direction, though she shunned more wholeheartedly than her sister the spiritualistic zeal which had flared up through the mother's determination to be in touch with her beloved and brilliantly attractive eldest son

[1] Lines prefixed to *Windlestraw, A Book of Verse* by Pamela Tennant, London, 1910.

Wyndham, who was killed in the Battle of the Somme in September 1916.

A letter to the sisters in the following January[1] reveals something other than the outwardly calm nature, the lover of the countryside and quietness, something which came, perhaps, from ancestry other than English[2] and was roused by grief to passionate, vibrant conviction of her dead son's living presence, yet beside her. Indeed the sayings of the young soldier in childhood, tinctured sometimes for his mother, even then, with clairvoyance, read later like foreknowledge. Mary used to muse on the sense of life's brevity and of the nearness of another world, which several young men of this time, among her acquaintance, seemed to possess, and she often wondered whether there were others with similar experience which, if collected, might reveal something unusual.

Charlotte Stewart's death in April 1918[3] was no heavier sorrow to Mary and Jane than the cruelly prolonged illness and decline of her powers which had weighed on their hearts for months which were now crawling into years, but the end brought a parting which seemed to involve so much of their lives, for she had been close as a sister and bound to them by links of shared tastes and associations since Lochearnhead days. In the summer they went to Ardvorlich Cottage to be with Charlotte's mother.

Almost with suddenness, finally the long tunnel of the First World War came to an end. The Findlaters shared acutely the high hopes of that time, and the deep apprehension about the future, though at first, it was naturally relief which dominated. The tremendous power of human beings for good became an absorbing thought. 'Perhaps,' wrote Mary, 'we shall all realize that more fully in the future, after seeing what ill will has been able to achieve.'[4]

[1] From 24 Queen Anne's Gate, 25th January, 1917.

[2] Her great-grandmother was Lady Edward Fitzgerald, the daughter of Madame de Genlis, and, it was conjectured, of Philip Égalité.

[3] 13th April, 1918.

[4] Letter to Marion Cadell, 10th November, 1918.

With the lifting of the war clouds, Mary and Jane almost immediately turned their attention to writing. Mention of a new book which they have on hand is made early in November 1918 and again towards the end of the month.

> We have got a few chapters done ... then waves of discouragement sweep over us & we are stuck fast for some days, & then start again. I don't know that it will ever be finished. Life's not so simple as it seems in the twenties, when you're in the fifties. So many complex sides of it turn up that often I wonder if it's any good trying to depict it at all. Yet it *interests* more & more.

The Findlaters were certainly not alone at that time in finding the fair prospect becoming suddenly bleak. A dark, cold winter drew down upon them, when 'fires were scarce'[1] and exhaustion with the ordinary business of life and fending for themselves were all too frequent. Many of their acquaintances were ill, some with the influenza which was sweeping across the country like a plague, and their beloved friend Agnes Kemp was dying. Mary and Jane began to wonder in a depressed fashion whether they could possibly manage to keep Southfield Mount, which they liked so much, going.

At this moment there came upon the scene a persuasive would-be buyer of the house. He was an ex-Serviceman who pleaded his great need of a home. The sisters allowed a kindly patriotism to weight the scales in favour of selling him the house. Reluctance to part with it was overcome by the satisfaction they felt in helping an ex-Serviceman to a home. Great was their chagrin, therefore, when a few days later they discovered that the purchaser had immediately resold the house for £100 more. Rather sheepishly he wrote offering to share some of the gains. Mary, however, replied somewhat haughtily that she and her sister had no wish to profit by his astuteness.

Fortunately they were after this able to rent Hatherleigh, another (for them far less attractive) house in Paignton. From this

---

[1] Summary Diary, November 1918.

base they searched for something more suitable, going as far afield as Rye. However, the lease of Hatherleigh was extended and they thankfully remained there for the time being, although they had no study to work in. It was in the dining-room of Hatherleigh that most of *Beneath the Visiting Moon* was written, and the letters to their friends, for, like their mother, they valued friendship supremely.

When the Findlaters heard of the prospect of Lord Grey's visit to America on a special mission connected with the Peace,[1] Mary wrote to him, full of hope and enthusiasm. Lord Grey replied from Fallodon on August 17th, 1919,

Dear Miss Findlater,

That thought of all the varied experience of life bearing fruit in an hour of supreme opportunity is a very good one, though I fear it may not be applicable to my visit to Washington.

I do feel that the experience of life is not lost; one grows by it continually, but after a certain time one feels that it is valuable as something which one will carry on to another existence rather than as something which is going to produce outward results here.

I remember very well about Charlotte Stewart and her illness. Surely it is a good preparation for the beauty of another world to appreciate the beauty of this, and her death, no doubt, is a loss to you and not to her, except in so far as any separation must be a loss to both.

My eyes have failed so much that, though they still serve me for such purposes as walking about, they cut one off from the pleasures of sight, such as flowers, and sunsets and beauty of landscape and pictures and people's faces. That, of course, makes life more of retrospect. One gets pleasure from walking in old places that revive memories. One is indifferent to new

[1] Lord Grey sailed to America in September 1919 'on a special mission to deal with questions arising out of the Peace, pending the appointment of a personal Ambassador'. Mainly because of the President's increasing illness and through no fault of Grey's, the mission was doomed to failure. v. G. M. Trevelyan, *Grey of Fallodon*, 1937, pp. 351 et seq.

scenes, because one gets nothing from them . . .

It implied no slackening of their devotion to the memory of Dorothy Grey, when two years later Mary and Jane rejoiced at their friend's engagement to the now widowed Lady Glenconner. Lord Grey wrote to Mary on 10th November, 1921,

> We did not mean to make any announcement now because it is too soon to speak of marriage yet and for the present things are remaining as they are. But new happiness has come into my life and I thank you very much for your letter. It expresses, too, some thoughts that are present in my own mind.

Lord Grey had been specially pleased with what he told Mary was the only 'original' remark that had been made to him about his engagement. Thinking of the first, great love of his life, and the new love which had now come into it, Mary had written that it was such a mistake to suppose that love was like a pound of tea so that what you gave to one you took from another.[1]

Fond as they were of Pamela Glenconner and highly as they esteemed Lord Grey, Mary and Jane put neither into quite the same rank as Dorothy Widdrington, the first Lady Grey, who remained always for them first in honour as in affection. In their eyes she possessed some inestimable quality, which raised her just above the level of other mortals, though this did not make her unhuman. Mary, who particularly disliked fulsome admiration, once remarked to me that 'Henry Newbolt's lines'[2] were 'perhaps a little exaggerated'. She had no doubt of his sincerity, nor (I knew well) considered her friend undeserving of high praise, but I think she felt that the simplicity of plain truth was alone worthy of her.

House hunting now became a preoccupation. Increasingly the Findlaters were directing their search towards Rye, but with no satisfactory results. In the intervals they were reading the Life of General Booth.

[1] Told me by Mary Findlater.

[2] Henry Newbolt. *Poems New and Old* London, 1912, p. 145. *On the Death of a Noble Lady.*

Wonderful old man! He had almost no sympathy with any beautiful, good or interesting side of life, as we know life; his very being was consumed away with a sort of mania of pity for the people of the under world, & for what he called 'saving souls'. You can't help getting fond of him before the end, in spite of everything. Life was one long, scarcely interrupted, noisy evangelist meeting from his boyhood till his death! How anyone could ever endure it & remain sane is extraordinary. I wish you were beside us to talk about it . . .[1]

A week or so later Mary and Jane were reading Henry James' letters. Mary describes these as 'often profoundly interesting' and adds:

It was queer reading them along with the Booth Life. They represented the two extremes of living. On the whole I *think* (I'm not quite sure) that General Booth's – no – it couldn't be! 'Saving souls' from morning to night by means of a hectoring doctrine of Hell fire & 'The Blood of the Lamb' *couldn't* be the purpose of the Creator, so perhaps H.J's feeling that to have written 'a little book of perfect short tales was work enough for a life time' is nearer the truth? . . .

This is a roasting hot morning again. The House Cleaning still splashing on its way with pails of soap and water everywhere, an upholstress working in the Garden House & Bunder in a towering passion over some trifle, tearing green gooseberries off the bushes as if they were scorpions.[2]

In idyllic weather during that summer of 1920, the Findlaters went to stay in Rye. One day of supreme peace and beauty was spent at Bodiam. Otherwise the search for houses was the chief object of any expedition and Mary was considerably occupied with an uncongenial little story which she was writing with Kate Riggs. The partnership was not as easy as it used to be,

I have finished half of my part in the silly book we began to

[1] Letter to Marion Cadell, 18th May, 1920.
[2] Letter to Marion Cadell, 26th May, 1920.

write with Kate Riggs last Autumn, & got it sent off, which
relieves me of an irksome task.

Dear Kate is an Angel, but an Angel with no taste in adjec-
tives, & if I have ever by any luck achieved one that is
descriptive she always deletes it & carefully substitutes the old,
old, well worn one that has jogged along with its noun since
the beginning. . . .
Rye is full of people, some exquisitely queer. I saw a creature
last week who seemed clothed only in in a brief chemise of
grey stockingnette, *quite* transparent & a rose-red hat. As she
twittered along on her stilt-like heels she made quite a sensation
even here. Also we met dear Ellen Terry, old, vague, & shabby
as a charwoman, erring along the High St. on her way, she said,
to see 'dear Winchelsea' and the cottage where she used to live.
A sad sight – but did you notice that the Empress Eugenie said,
'*Il ne faut pas dramatizer la vie – c'est assez dramatique*' or words
to that effect. Perhaps Ellen Terry is wiser not to be too
sentimental & to revisit the glimpses of the moon. Still it's
sad to see her there.[1]

The attraction of Rye increased, nor suffered any diminution
through the disappointment of being unable to afford that
summer the usual visit to Scotland. But the Findlaters now felt
doomed to Paignton and to a house there

not nearly as nice as Southfield . . . struggling to get away
seems of no use, we only sink deeper, like the fly in treacle.
All that we can do is to quiet ourselves with the belief that
there is some good reason for it.

Victoria Cholmondeley was with us for two days, spent by
her mostly in bed, poor dear, as she arrived quite knocked up.
We sat beside her and talked . . . something of her lovely
serenity & strength of faith cheered us on even after she
had left. She simply goes *with* the stream of events in the
calm assurance that it is the best, & the right things will
all come if we wait 'as the eyes of an handmaid wait on the

[1] Mary to Marion Cadell, 20th July, 1920.

hand of her mistress'. *She is right*, I'm sure, if only we can do it.[1]

In London, before finally returning to Paignton, Mary was again impressed by 'Dear V. Cholmondeley' because she always seems to possess the eternal peace, more than anyone else we know ... Both she & Mary looked ill ... They are anxious about Diana & are tightened about money (like the rest of us) & the new house struck us as not at all so pleasing as Leonard Place.[2]

In her letters to Marion Cadell at this time, Mary reveals something of her desire and effort to attain 'inner peace', a state more immune from outward circumstances. As best they might, the sisters settled down to life in Paignton, but they found it 'stuffier and duller' than before and too remote from their friends. However, they wrote.

'It is necessary to existence in this place,' Mary maintained; nor were she and Jane aloof from surroundings or untouched by what was going on.

This has been an exquisite golden day [she wrote to Marion Cadell on Armistice Day, 1920] like an iced summer day ... In the morning we went to Church early for the Armistice Service, at the hour when the 'Unknown Warrior' was being take to the Abbey.

There wasn't much in the Service as the prayers were mostly inaudible & the music very indifferent, but as we came down the great old Church I saw how almost every face was ravaged by grief. The five years of the war have made havoc indeed with the people who used to come to this Church! Nearly everyone we knew there had lost someone.

Now Jeanie & I, rolled up in our duvets, are writing in the funny shaped little dining-room, our lamp on the oak chest in the 'Chippendale' window ... This afternoon we walked

[1] Mary to Marion Cadell, 9th September, 1920.

[2] In 1919 the Cholmondeleys had moved from 2 Leonard Place to 4 Argyll Road, Kensington.

all 'three Miss Gribbles' up the high lanes behind Southfield & saw the sea very blue & calm below. The oaks have all turned the colour of brass, the fields are green still . . . The whole country was flooded with sun & seemed a goodly land indeed. We ought to be pleased in such heavenly weather, even if we have to live in Paignton for the rest of our days.

During the winter that followed, Mary and Jane wrote their novel *Beneath the Visiting Moon* in the little dining-room, at *Hatherleigh*, while January storms raged outside and February came in bitterly cold. It was not until mid-April that the book was finished 'with great exhaustion'.[1]

This was the period when they were seeing much of Ella Christie[2] whom they had met for the first time in the autumn of 1918. Mary writes of her to Marion Cadell:

I wish we had been there when Miss Christie arrived to watch her interest & pleasure in everything . . . We owe her a real debt of gratitude for sending us *Arabia Deserta* (from the Geographical Library), it has given us intense pleasure — more than a book — it seems really as if one had been transported on some magic carpet to the midst of the Arabian Desert, & had eaten dates & swayed on camels & sat in the 'Houses of Hair' until we awoke with a start to find it was a dream, & that life in Paignton was reality. Gracious! how sick I am of it!

Later she adds,

We've been entertaining the Robert Simpsons (Free High Church) all afternoon — quite refreshing to talk with intelligent people from Scotland . . .

and puts in a more cheerful bit of news:

Jane has just been asked to send one of her Scots stories for

[1] Summary Diary, 15th April, 1922.
[2] ibid., 13th September, 1918, and 29th July, 1922.

Jane and Mary
A drawing by Lady Jane Lindsay

inclusion in the 'Best Short Stories of the World' which is coming out soon. Kipling, Hardy, etc: 'Set her up'.[1]

The possibility of building a house at Rye was now being considered. Negotiations were prolonged, progress slow, disappointments numerous throughout the spring of 1923, when Mary and Jane were correcting proofs of *Beneath the Visiting Moon*. At last, however, in May, difficulties were cleared up and an agreement signed. The prospect was suddenly full of hope. They were going to leave Paignton and live in the place of their choice, in a neighbourhood they really liked. Then, as suddenly, the skies were darkened by direful apprehension. Mary, who had not been feeling well for some time (even the tone of the Summary Diary reflects this and her frequent mention of weariness or exhaustion endorses it) became ill. Expert opinion was sought and an exploratory operation gave cause for real alarm.

That summer she underwent three operations, one of which was for internal cancer. In later years, to bring hope to others, she liked to tell how an old lady, previously unknown to her, who had happened to hear of her plight, had come expressly to tell her of her own apparently miraculous recovery from the same condition after a major operation many years previously. Just before she took the anaesthetic, the surgeon asked Mary, 'Do you *want* to live?' and she replied, with great emphasis, '*Passionately!*' 'Then,' said he with conviction ringing in his voice, 'you will.'

[1] Letter to Marion Cadell of 23rd November, 1922. This collection was in fact *31 Stories by Thirty and One Authors*, ed. Ernest Rhys and Catherine A. Dawson Scott, New York, 1923. Hardy and Kipling were not contributors, but G. K. Chesterton, John Galsworthy, and H. G. Wells were.

6

Rye and Comrie

Mary's strong will to live was reinforced by excitement and joy in building the house at Rye. It was situated just above the military road, looking out over the distant railway (from which it could easily be seen) to the flats, the sea and the sky beyond. It was a view extending apparently to infinity, an aspect often radiant with sunlight. The colder back of the house was screened from the north by a high bank.

Even Mora's habitual fears were subdued temporarily by the attraction for her of a place which provided so many subjects and possibilities for the sketching she loved and in which she now showed some talent above the ordinary.

There were delays, worries, anxieties. It was a big financial venture for the Findlaters, but inwardly and outwardly they had never been reconciled to Devonshire. Paignton, which they found less alien than Torquay, was far from being the home of their hearts. At Rye they came to the happiest period of their lives.

By the mid-nineteen twenties the day of their books was practically over, but they still had their devoted readers and still retained a place in the estimation of the literary *èlite*. In reply to an appreciative letter from Mary, Virginia Woolf wrote in her delicate, pointed hand,

> 52, Tavistock Sqre
> London, W.C.1
> 22nd October 1927.

Dear Miss Findlater
This is most kind of you & your sister to write to me, & if all letters gave me as much pleasure as yours I should certainly

not complain of having to answer them.[1] I am particularly glad to think that writers whose work I admire should find anything to please them in mine.

When I write another novel I shall remember your kind words which will encourage me to try to do better next time.

Please thank your sister for me.

        & believe me
            Yours sincerely
                Virginia Woolf.[2]

Similarly, a few years earlier,[3] De la Mare had written to Jane that he wished he could express exactly the kind of degree of pleasure which her letter had given him.

But you know what a rare joy such things are & from a fellow craftsman, & how difficult it is to say anything in return. But I do think it is immensely kind of you to write. Will it sound like sour grapes if I say that it isn't wholly a disappointment that the book hasn't greened Ethel Dell with jealousy. When one slays one's tens of thousands no doubt vanity adjusts the scene! But she can't have any real exercise over the Memoirs[4] – though more copies have edged out than seemed the least likely.

I should feel sadder – much sadder to hear that you were bidding the very queer being farewell, if I believed that could be true. . . .

From poverty stricken daughters of a remote Scottish manse, the Findlaters had become, through their writing, comfortably self-supporting, and as individuals, known, respected and loved by many of the distinguished and best among their contemporaries.

---

[1] Cf. *A Writer's Diary*, London, 1953, p. 116. 'I get letter after letter about my books and they scarcely please me.'

[2] Even these few lines reduced the writer's slender reserve of energy that afternoon, for she writes, alluding to *Orlando* 'This is a book . . . which I write after tea. And my brain was full of ideas, but I have spent them on Mr. Ashcroft and Miss Findlater, fervent admirers. *A Writer's Diary*, p. 116.

[3] 23rd November, 1921, from Rodmell in Sussex.

[4] *Memoirs of a Midget.*

They possessed their own house, a state of affairs which they considered extremely important for a woman's happiness, were she married or single. It was built and very largely furnished on the proceeds of their well-earned money. There they could entertain the friends who meant so much to them and there they were surrounded by books, old and new, piled to the ceiling in their study where Dr. Abercrombie's[1] great bookcase fitted exactly along one side of the room.

Beautiful places, beautiful things in simplicity and good order were very dear to Mary and Jane, and Mary loved old furniture with the discrimination of a connoisseur. She would vanish from beside a slightly bewildered companion if she caught sight of so much as a wooden leg of elegant line amid a medley of dull ugly pieces, or cause her prize to be extracted laboriously from beneath piles of mattresses, new chairs and bamboo tables till it emerged like a queen from exile, some gem absolutely right for the new little dining-hall. Or it might be a bit of old china that attracted her, 'cream-coloured . . . slightly tanned by age and ovens, with a tiny band of gilded leaves and a narrow coral edge . . . shape . . . like a pineapple with half of it a lid that lifts off . . . to any seeing eye it has a suggestion of antique cosiness that is most appealing.' The sisters concluded that it was the very dish from which Mr. Woodhouse refused a hot muffin on that celebrated evening when he suggested a little gruel all round.

If, however, it became a question of people or things, people were put first, at whatever cost.

> our darling little Donovan girls arrived, flushed with excitement, carrying a big parcel — their own handiwork — *a painted lamp shade* for our room. Jane, of course, did and said the proper thing, & I quickly swallowed a moment of dismay, & took them up, & they stood breathless whilst the plain parchment one was taken off, and theirs put on. Then there were sighs of satisfaction, & much admiration from the dismayed recipients.

---

[1] Dr. John Abercrombie, 1780–1844, author of *Enquiry Concerning the Intellectual Powers*. The bookcase was a legacy from his sisters.

It will last for years & hangs in front of our window & can be seen from the road, so any attempt to place it elsewhere would be instantly found out, The blessed little things must have laboured so valiantly at it & it's a wonderful piece of work for children of their age. We do indeed appreciate it – if only there hadn't been quite so much gimp about the edges! But a gift 'with much love' from children is better than taste.[1]

Jane liked children, Mary was fond of individual ones, and the sisters had several special friends among the small boys and girls of the families around. They both loved people, though with discrimination. They found some excessively tedious. Occasionally, they used to amuse themselves by making up, in imagination, a tea-party of all the prize bores they knew. Mary could ill brook fools. Jane was more patient. Even in Rye they sometimes found themselves 'feeding the sparrows' (a phrase they used for inroads on time made by mentally trivial people) but they had many real friends there.

Dorothy Carter, who out of untold difficulty and adversity, launched a successful career for herself as a maker of delicious and subsequently world-famous marmalade, was a heroine in their eyes. There were the Luxmoores, who became friends for life; the Rendels of Owley, a house so old that it was said to have been built originally without chimneys. Mary and Jane wished that these friends of the 'Peasemarsh Colony' or 'Simple-Lifers', as the Findlaters called them, lived within easier reach, but the sisters kept open house (usually on Sundays when their maid was out) and there were many agreeable, convivial Sunday teas, when Bunder's scones and cakes were consumed, 'the youngest of the party' washed up and every topic in heaven and earth was discussed.

There was a series of pet cats at The Roundel Gate, as the Findlaters called their house, cats who became human inmates and very much members of the household, whether they chose to reside mainly on the kitchen hearth or by the study

[1] Letter to Marion Cadell. 10th January, 1932.

fire. Individuality and intelligence were preferred to breeding. Anything too delicately nurtured and man-made was at a discount.

The Findlaters' horizon was not bounded by matters domestic, nor was it even restricted to their friends. They were interested in the affairs of Rye and especially in the efforts to control the mosquito menace there. They were amused (perhaps a little gratified) to know that a local inhabitant, considered by them to be a wrongdoer, would slip off down a side lane, rather than face the Miss Findlaters, if he saw them looming in the distance. They kept in touch with new writers and new writing, they keenly watched the early development of the B.B.C. Jane broadcast a talk on gipsies. Mary, who found that her style stiffened in pen and ink as her face at a photographers, preferred spoken narrative when she wanted to tell a good story. Various circumstances, however, including increasing deafness which made it impossible for her to hear the sound of her own voice, conspired to prevent her attempting to broadcast. She might have been a little intractable. She had no illusions about the B.B.C.

> I do feel now as if the whole world, & all its present history, is being boiled down into an unctuous B.B.C. Broth — or as if an immense-voiced, common-minded sort of gargantuan Governess had control of the news we are allowed to hear & was telling us even what we had to think about it. Yet how good some of it is! I know we should hate not to have it now.

For all the idyllic qualities of the Rye period, inevitably there fell across it those shadows which darken with a browner tinge advancing years. There was the loss of their sister Mora, after sad illness, and of beloved and faithful friends, including their dear tyrant of the kitchen, Bunder; there was the farewell to Mrs. Stewart at Ardvorlich. They had found her so much restored in a setting of domestic contentment and it was only the slight tremor of the leaf-like, frail hand on Mary's arm as the brave good-byes were said, that left the guest knowing that this was the last time. Mary went away through the radiant autumn afternoon along the road beside Loch Earn, with *Look thy last on all things lovely every hour* echoing perpetually in her heart.

The sisters kept up with Lord Grey throughout the tragedies, losses and infirmities of his later years, and judging from his replies, their letters brought him some grains of comfort, and even a little pleasure. There was one friend for whom sorrow and mourning seemed incongruous. Her life, her death, her very illnesses were so illumined by the inner light which overflowed in loving kindness, yet seemed to set her apart from other human beings, that her friends were sent away not sorrowful but rejoicing. Victoria Cholmondeley had written to Mary and Jane at Bunder's death with great sympathy but with absolute confidence in the fullness of life of 'that other world',

> You will say, 'How do you know that?' I can only say, 18 months ago when I so nearly went over myself, I saw and felt enough of 'The Protective Greatness' that so nearly engulfed me – that for long after . . . & indeed I still feel . . . it was *the great opportunity missed*.
> It still comforts me to think of it lying there, ready to take us when the moment comes.

The Findlaters did not ceaselessly mourn old friendships or try to live in the past. They forged new links with the younger generation and letters would have continued to flow between them and Victoria Cholmondeley's niece, Stella Benson, had it not been for her early death. But there were others, and there was still the circle at 39 Harrington Gardens where Mary and Jane often stayed and always found mental and spiritual stimulus. The Inges were often there and Rowland Corbet who possessed 'a sweet attractive kind of grace' (not an unfailing endowment of all mystics) and his approach to questions of faith and belief at once appealed to minds formed by the influence of an enlightened Calvanism and the magnificent opening sentences of the Shorter Catechism. But Mary and Jane had no use for hot-house religiosity and were far from idolizing any spiritual directors. A suggestion of female intensity drew from them a wholesome chuckle or an astringent comment.

They had not lost the independence of thought which had caused them to 'treat rough' on the mental level, their father's raw and sometimes rather helpless young assistants, but they had travelled a long way from some of the beliefs and notions in which they had been brought up. Nevertheless there was no violent repudiation of their traditions. The new was grafted on to the old, the trammels imposed upon their youthful minds fell away, like husks whose work was done, and the sisters determined on nothing so much as the prevention of any tendency in themselves to dry up or become rigid mentally as the years went by. 'While we're here let us love one another more than ever, for nothing else is worth living for',[1] sums up the Findlaters' feelings towards their inner circle of friends. Here was the pivot of their world, but there were many other things which combined to make it for them.

As I escorted Jane to the gate just now, the world (at peace) and Rye in the pink twilight with the lights beginning in the town & the pale fields below did seem a pretty good place to come back to.

How cheerful our daily world really is. 'There are worse things than dulness,' as Mrs. Minniver wrote in *The Times* after the crisis.[2]

So wrote Mary of their surroundings and life.[3] Some while earlier she had confessed 'though I shall be seventy in about a fortnight now, I still find this various and delightful world well worth living in.'[4]

Jane's few amusing, racy letters to Marion Cadell, recounting the small happenings, incongruities and absurdities of Rye society,

---

[1] Letter to Marion Cadell, 31st November, 1934.

[2] *The Times*, Thursday, 6th October, 1938, p. 15, article entitled *Back to Normal*. 'Another thing people had gained was an appreciation of the value of dulness.'

[3] Letter to Marion Cadell, 19th October, 1938.

[4] Letter to Marion Cadell, 11th February, 1935.

Jane and Mary at The House of Ross, Comrie, Perthshire
Jane and Mary at Earn Hope, Comrie, Perthshire

spiced with one or two minor scandals, reveal her zest and pleasure in the human entertainment that village life can afford. For all its trials, some illnesses and some financial worries, together with the normal vicissitudes of human life, this decade and a half was the equivalent of the 'lived happily ever after' ending of the fairy-tale, or of an old-fashioned novel. 'That perfect time was a jewel in the story of your life,' wrote Lady Jane Lindsay to Mary, years later.[1]

But the clouds were gathering. This time, long before the storm broke, the Findlaters, like some of their compatriots, were very much aware of the darkening horizon. The sisters lived through 'Munich' in acute anxiety and enjoyed the transient untold relief which followed. Then their little affairs, as Mary would often say, were caught up in the great wheel of the world's misfortune. By 1940 it became clear that Jane's heart trouble was increasingly menacing and as enemy aggression became nearer and more noisy, the sisters reluctantly decided that they must leave Rye, for the time being at least. They travelled up to Perthshire in the summer of 1940,[2] little supposing that they would never see Rye again.

Mary often spoke of the Fate, apparently so cruel and perverse, which drove them from their small paradise, but she would add that out of all the great griefs and upheavals of the Second World War, what appeared to be their own little tragedy proved a blessing, however heavily disguised at first.

They went back to the country of their childhood, to Comrie, within a few miles of Lochearnhead where they had grown up and where Mary herself was born. They stayed in various lodgings and as far as wartime would permit were fairly happy in most of them, but sorely missed their beloved house at Rye.

The Maclagans were near them, the Cadells and Margaret Roberton were within much easier reach. Other friends seemed to spring from the very soil around them. Many were most

[1] Letter written from Hedingham Castle, Halsted, Essex, 16th September 1946.

[2] Summary Diary, Summer 1940.

affectionately regarded, all were included in a mental panorama which might have furnished a large and comfortable novel. Shades of idiosyncrasy, tiny outward indications of manner, in a detail of appearance or dress, in a trick of speech, any of which might betray character, were carefully noted and mentally cherished.

There were ups and downs during those war years. The sisters followed the course of events closely, anxiously. There were wartime distresses and miseries, hard winters, illnesses, once more some money anxieties and the pinch of poverty. But nothing was overwhelming while they had 'friends and each other'.[1] It was now more than ten years since the strange panic (which had first seized them as children on the hillside at Edenchip) recurred. Again the sisters were alone, but this time standing beneath a towering rock, one of those weirdly shaped, dark, menacing cliff faces of Skye. As they gazed at its black, implacable surface, they were swept by an overwhelming sense of inevitability which included that of their own parting in the unrelenting course of time. Childish flight was no remedy, but as they stood frozen with fear and grief, they found themselves crying, crying like the ancients who wept at horror in the face of Mediterranean storms or monstrous portents. Tears brought release, the shadow passed, but the experience was not forgotten.

With the infinite relief they felt in the cessation of fighting came a new anxiety. Jane's heart condition became worse, markedly reducing her powers of getting about and her total strength. A premonition (such as her father had experienced) of the approaching Presence assailed Jane's thought and communicated itself to Mary.

In the first pages of Jane's diary for that year I find she wrote some words from a book of Siegfried Sassoon's — 'His life renouncing eyes'. I remember her own eyes as she quoted them to me. I think she knew I knew what she meant, but we said nothing about that at the moment. The whole month of January was a long struggle with illness.[2]

[1] Letter to Marion Cadell, Christmas Day, 1945.
[2] Summary Diary, January 1946.

It was the shadow of shadows, the Inevitable that they had dreaded in nightmare panic on the hillside as children and in the towering, crushing mass of the black wall of rock looming above them in Skye, as a symbol of the Implacable.

January merged into February, and with a lovely springlike March, unusually warm and sunny, matters improved. On 18th May Jane notes in her diary, 'Began to read *Arabia Deserta* – read until my eyes ached – a splendid day of outside sunshine.' Maybe the order and emphasis of the last two words were pure chance, or had she a sense that 'the bright day' was not for her? That night came a severe heart attack. On the following day[1] in merciful unconsciousness, gently, as she had lived, Jane slipped away.

The last words that Mary thought she heard her murmur seemed to run like a bright thread through the far past at Lochearnhead, the questing middle years of writing and fame, the present stress, the future, gathering and binding them together into one shining ring of words, '. . . shall not walk in darkness, but shall have the light of life.'

Mary fully believed that she could survive Jane for little more than a few months, at most a few years, but the intensity of her passion for life and interest in it seemed, even after this crushing loss, to bear her almost unwilling, sometimes despairing conscious self through the first depths, slowly, painfully, but unrelentingly back to life, and back even to a measure of happiness, love and friendship aiding. A house in Comrie, and some of her own possessions round her, the Maclagans, her 'Guardian Angels' as she called them, living now only across the two adjoining gardens, helped the recovery. But naturally life could never be the same, and now old age was to be faced with, eventually semi-blindness, and deafness which finally defied all hearing aids. Before these infirmities reached their most acute stage, Mary would read aloud to Nan and Haya Maclagan with that peculiar power of vocal interpretation which is sometimes the gift of the rare and comprehending mind. Later she would repeat long

[1] 20th May, 1946.

passages from some specially loved poem or prose work, returning most often to Jane's favourite, *Pilgrim's Progress*, especially the episode at Doubting Castle, for she liked to dwell upon the incident of the liberating key which was in Christian's possession all the time, and she would repeat Hopeful's 'Who knows but that God that made the world may cause that Giant Despair may die . . .'

Despite increasing handicaps of age, and of deafness in particular, the old delight of posing tough questions sparked into life again, especially under the stimulus of a visit from priest or minister. On such occasions one could not help recalling those Sundays at Lochearnhead when Mary and Jane used to put the preacher through his paces before the service.

From her sofa at Four Hollies she would greet the entering guest, or perhaps would wait until he was seated beside her, already slightly embarrassed by the end of what looked like a telephone line, or whatever form was taken by the current hearing aid. It was never long before she fired her first shot.

Mr. — I have prepared a question for you . . .
Here is a good subject for a sermon. Don't you think you should tackle this . . .?

Her questions were not designed to tease or merely to puzzle. Generally they were asked in perfect good faith and in a spirit of honest inquiry. Nevertheless, one sensed that whether they probed deep, or simply shed a bizarre light on some dusty long-shelved problem, the flicker of a wince on the part of the visitor added spice and saved the hostess from boredom, if she had drawn a blank and interesting discussion were not to follow.

It was as I sat beside her in the drawing-room at Four Hollies (where everything was old and shabby but antique and graceful) that Mary Findlater told me much of this story. It was a room into which sunlight often poured, and by warm summer twilight or by the fire in winter, we would settle down to the intricacies of many a tale to beguile the evening. Each would be skilfully and perfectly woven, every thread was in place, however complicated the design and brought with unbroken certainty to the finishing point.

Mary's dark eyes, her soft, snowy white hair, the exquisitely-cut, small aquiline features, the intelligence which shone from her face made her a fascinating *raconteuse*. Even the slightly rasping 'deaf voice' was not unpleasing while it was sensitively attuned to the changing mood of her story, long or short, modulating to the key of tragedy or comedy, expressing every shade of emotion. The longer stories were, on the whole, the most enthralling. One felt almost cheated if they were brief, however effective and concentrated.

Those which pieced into the story of her life and Jane's have been put together in this book, supported by other evidence, in the hope that a few readers may find something here which is yet 'remarkable beneath the visiting moon'.

7

Novels and Stories

Between them Mary and Jane Findlater produced twenty-three books. In two of this total they collaborated with friends.[1] Mary wrote six novels alone and Jane five, though a long short story, *A Green Grass Widow*, might be added to her list. They wrote three novels together, *Crossriggs* (1908), *Penny Monypenny* (1911) and *Beneath the Visiting Moon* (1923) and an amusing little book of advice from experience in living the simple life in wartime called *Content with Flies* (1916).

Mary's earliest publication was a small collection of poems entitled *Songs and Sonnets* published in 1895 shortly before Jane's first novel, *The Green Graves of Balgowrie* (1896). Both sisters wrote short stories and here Jane was much the more prolific of the two. Some of these were collected. *Tales that are Told* (1901) and *Seen and Heard Before and After 1914* (1916) were joint publications. *Seven Scots Stories* (1912) and *A Green Grass Widow and Other Stories* (1921) were by Jane alone. She wrote numbers of short stories which were not collected and which appeared in periodicals; similarly essays, some of which were published together in *Stones from a Glass House* (1904).

Realistic characterization, especially of their own compatriots, is constant, but although they are never shallow in their approach, depth, originality and artistry vary. By Mary these are best sustained in her novel *The Rose of Joy* (1903) by Jane in her *Rachel* (1899) and in her first book, *The Green Graves of Balgowrie* (1896). The novels written with Kate Riggs and 'Allan McAulay' (the Findlaters' friend, Charlotte Stewart) served their day, but little

[1] *The Affair at the Inn,* 1904, and *Robinetta,* 1911, both with Kate Douglas Wiggin and Allan McAulay.

more. Those written by the sisters together reach their highest level. *Crossriggs* has been generally considered their best work. *Penny Monypenny* and *Beneath the Visiting Moon* were adequate successors for the quality is steadier in these three. It is never of the first order, at least not upon the grand scale, though critics and admirers have made high claims for *Crossriggs*. In their other novels the true light comes and goes, but always there is evidence of its presence, of some comprehensive view of human life and of the ability to present it in terms of reality. Suitably modified, these generalizations apply to the short stories and to Jane's Essays, though in neither of these categories is there such variation of standard as in the novels, and Jane's Gipsy stories contain some of her best, most sympathetic and realistic writing. She had not, like George Borrow, lived among gipsies, but the keenest observation has gone into this work. Contemporary critics loudly praised the author's clear-eyed approach.

To generalize a little further, Jane was more interested than Mary in the child outlook and the primitive mind. Her nature, both in life and art, leant in the direction of the tragic, though she could write a gay short story and possessed a quick sense of humour. Mary's bent was towards comedy of manners, though not exclusively so, and her characters consequently were more restricted to types familiar to her among the middle classes, 'the county' and their retainers.

The Findlater stories and novels are unpretentious, simple narratives, not constructed from any exotic or subtle viewpoint, their sympathies are clearly engaged with heroine, hero and all the characters from 'mid-grey' to 'white'. None, of course, is absolutely white. To the darker shades of grey they are usually charitable, and beyond that there are few extremes. A certain kind of unmitigated, deep-seated vulgarity of nature (not vulgarity of manners) was their profound aversion. Their novels, in a word, are old-fashioned. They are leisurely in pace, but interestingly near in style to the spoken word. The voice of the narrator is distinctly audible from time to time. Story telling was one of the chief forms of entertainment at the Lochearnhead Manse, especially in winter. With Findlaters and Borthwicks it seems to have been in the family tradition and amounted to an art. In her eighties and nineties Mary Findlater was still a fascinating raconteuse.

Nearly always the sisters based their plots upon some actual occurrence or true story of which they knew. They seemed to find this a kind of support, although they were far from imagining that it would endow their work with the reality and convincing power which they knew full well could only be obtained by art. It was, however, a little amusing sometimes, especially in the earlier less sure days of authorship to watch a critic pompously denying the possibility of one of their plots[1] which was based upon the incognito visit to an elderly Edinburgh lady of a Russian Czar. This, however had happened to their Borthwick grandmother's governess. The chair on which the Czar sat was long preserved and cherished.

What the Findlaters did best, and what gave their novels their appeal can be conveniently illustrated from half a dozen of their literary works. Mary wrote poetry, mainly in her more youthful years, but the poetic feeling in Jane never found expression through verse. It is evident in her first book, *The Green Graves of Balgowrie*. This story was another family preserve, a legacy in fact of a rather insubstantial kind which included drawings and verses celebrating the old eighteenth-century house of Ballyeoman in Fifeshire, and letters to Mary's and Jane's mother from the woman who lived there and whose eccentricity is traced in its growth to madness, through the length of Jane's novel.

The events which occurred in the eighteen forties seemed to Jane, some fifty years later, rather too close in time for her mood and purpose. She, therefore, pushed them back into an earlier century, which lent them a certain dignity and remoteness and enabled her more appropriately to touch the bleak and terrible situation with pastoral charm. The only invented character

[1] Jane Findlater. *In Hopefield Square* from *Tales that are Told,* London 1902.

Doctor Cornelius Hallijohn, was a thoroughgoing eighteenth-century type, a cultured, half-sceptic minister, with drinking habits no worse than those of others of his profession at that time.

Indeed the big, handsome minister, kindly beneath a thin layer of cynicism, appears to stand for life and sanity, over against the inhuman, half-crazy Mrs. Marjoribanks. This woman was no ordinary family tyrant. She believed in a certain kind of freedom, but quite inflexibly. She had brought her two daughters to this lonely spot in order to carry out her theories to best advantage. It was a period of experimental education. Mrs. Marjoribanks read Voltaire and Hume. Education was her mania but it was not entirely restricted to the mind. With remarkable inconsistence she envisaged her daughters one day taking their place in the very society from which she had been at such pains to withdraw them and to fit them for this there was enacted every Thursday evening the strangest scene in the drawing-room at Balgowrie (Jane's name for the Ballyeoman of real life).

The two girls, garbed in 'curious sprigged muslins' would present themselves at the drawing-room door. There they found Mrs. Marjoribanks standing at one end of the room in the full evening dress of twenty years since. 'She advanced to meet them with a sweeping curtsey, while instructing them *sotto voce* to do the same. Then ensued introductions which were given at great length.'

Chairs represented the guests, and Mrs Marjoribanks would sweep up to one and make an elaborate introduction of her elder daughter, waving her gloved hand and producing more billowing curtsies. This performance was apt to strike the pupils so dumb that their instructress would imperiously indicate that conversation on the topics of the day must begin immediately, and the narrator comments, 'Surely the angels must have laughed, if they did not weep, to watch these ghostly receptions of bodiless guests, and listen to the talk that was carried on in the echoing old room.'

One girl supplied the music, shivering and nodding over the notes of the spinet, while the other danced and mopped and mowed to the chairs and the ottoman at her mother's command, until places were exchanged, the player danced and the dancer perched on the high stool before the spinet, and so on, during four weary hours.

It was a singular performance and at each reiteration a degree more so. The last fully described enactment is preluded in the novel by a little scene of dressing for the occasion, utterly individual in its colour and circumstances, but in its poise between the trivial and the tragic, between death and a bridal (never to take place), stirs memories of old ballads and old plays, the green willow song or the floating corpse of a flower-decked bride. The poetry which Jane would never attempt to write is in this book of hers.

Rachel is the study of a man with gifts of clairvoyance inherited from a gipsy mother, some mystical tendencies, ability to preach and impressive appearance, who is gradually and almost insensibly driven to abandon his real faith and doctrine for meretricious signs and wonders. The scene is set mainly in Edinburgh and strikingly reveals Jane's microscopic powers of observation. Some people thought Mary Findlater alarming. Very few considered Jane so, but the gifts displayed here make understandable the comment of a mutual friend who declared that Mary's forthrightness was much less daunting than Jane's silence and unspoken thought.

Mrs. Allan, the heroine Rachel's 'Cousin Elizabeth', is one of the line of formidable elderly women, often grimly religious, who frequent the sisters' books. Not seldom these oppressors take an Auntly form and in varying degree are drawn from the life. Models were close at hand for the two young novelists in the persons of Borthwick aunts or in the circle of their Edinburgh friends.

The writer is concerned in *Rachel* about the fate of cultivated young women, inheriting poverty with no future before them except marriage, or acting as the servant or somewhat crushed companion of some older wealthy woman, probably a relative. Although the solution in this novel is left in slight doubt, clearly the answer in the author's mind is the right husband or what promises to be a tolerably happy marriage. This is generally the solution of such a situation in the Findlaters' earlier novels. Later this conclusion is far from being the only one.

In Mary's *The Rose of Joy* the problem is debated between the heroine and her friends and the solution in the writer's mind is different. The story opens in a village just off 'the old road' from Edinburgh to London, with a meeting between a retired Indian army officer and the lady who once, long ago, refused to marry him. The ravages of age, especially as they had marked and changed the woman, are indicated with Thackerayan skill. Thereafter, many other personages and scenes are introduced, the solid well-to-do bourgeois household and the proud, 'high born beggars', typical among Scottish upper-class families and depicted by the Findlaters in their last book in the final stages of decadence. In *The Rose of Joy*, however, they are endowed with some finer qualities, though there is no sparing of harsh realism even here.

In this book tragedy is blent with comedy almost at every turn. The heroine, 'a little white shabby bride in a local dress' never loses her strange apartness throughout a drawing-room wedding where she is an actor in such a milieu and among such absurdities as would have graced the more hilarious *Experiences of an Irish R.M.* This was a favourite method, which Mary used both in the stories she wrote and in those she loved to relate to a sympathetic listener. Nowhere does she stretch the tension between comedy and tragedy so near to breaking point, yet so effectively, as in *The Rose of Joy*.

Attempts were often made and amusement derived from guessing which sister contributed what in the novels of collaboration. They themselves occasionally aided and abetted such speculation and even confessed that one or other was responsible for this or that. But in the main it was complete collaboration by personalities in close and harmonious relationship. There are no seams or joins visible in the three novels written by Mary and Jane together. It was in effect the writing of one person.

Crossriggs was depicted as a village only an hour by train from

Edinburgh, yet after a day in the city it was the custom when alighting at the village station to draw a deep breath with the exclamation, 'How good the air tastes after being in town.'

The very circumstantial description of the village suggested to many readers a real place, and very frequent were the speculations as to this. Ormiston in character and situation came exceedingly near the mark. Mary Findlater, in after years, would never absolutely confirm this origin. There was perhaps a touch of the composite and the imaginary in Crossriggs, although it was most like Ormiston.

The authoresses began *Crossriggs* in the manner that was natural to them.

Romance, I think, is like the rainbow, always a little away from the place where you stand. So the old days at Crossriggs may have been more interesting than the present — perhaps it is only the distance of years that makes the picture so vivid.

In characteristic leisurely fashion the tellers wind their way into the story and the reader, though permitted to become less and less aware of their presence, is never allowed absolutely to forget it. The sisters' voices blend so that the tone is of one voice, colouring the narrative with its own amusement, sorrow, exasperation, likes and dislikes. Through the guise of reminiscence the voice speaks directly to the reader, consciously evoking his response, and if he accepts it, this manner becomes the charm of the book. For instance, alluding to Robert Maitland's marriage,

The Maitland's only child had died some years before they came to settle in Crossriggs. Mrs Maitland may have been sorry about that, because she never took the slightest notice of other children, or made any allusion to the loss of their own ... 'That child must have been imported,' Alex would say. 'I don't believe she ever had it!'
Laura Maitland regarded her husband as a mere attribute of herself, taking a kind of satisfaction in his charm, his success — much as she did in her clothes or her house ...

Well, out of the whole world of women, Robert had chosen and married her, so presumably there must have been something he admired in her.... Whatever he felt about his marriage, he presented the same happy behaviour, and it was only an old friend who could notice the change that, like a frost in the night, had turned summer into autumn without a sound.[1]

As the novel gathers momentum, such passages are less frequent. There is little or no turning aside or slowing down of the pace for comment, after the early chapters, although the illusion of a tale remembered and told is never quite lost. Discursive and meandering enough, as it might appear to a later generation of readers, *Crossriggs* possesses certain advantages in being concentrated within the circle of a village or small provincial town. The society is Scottish but not markedly so, and the fact that reviewers particularly noted this[2] supports one's conviction that the authoresses had grasped much that was permanent and universal in such a community.

The characters belong almost exclusively to the upper- and middle-class of society, which were strata more clearly distinguishable in those days than now. They are among the best and most alive ever invented by the two sisters.

Reviewers bandy about the terms 'hero' and 'heroine'. They incline to the view that there is no hero in *Crossriggs*. It is, however, surely true that middle-class comedy, or tragi-comedy is soil in which heroines rather than heroes grow, and that masculine heroic dimensions hardly fit into such a frame. Moreover, the male reviewer can lose his heart to the heroine and be carried away by the tender passion, whereas for him, the process of identification with a hero is bound to be a more deliberate and calculated affair throughout. Women's heroes have often failed to satisfy the critical male. On the whole he did not take to Robert Maitland, but contemporary women readers sighed over him and found that he was 'so like Professor —' that they were positive the Miss

[1] *Crossriggs* pp. 16–17.

[2] *Spectator,* 18th April, 1908, p. 624. *Athenaeum,* 16th May, 1908.

Findlaters must have had 'him' in mind. In fact, that character goes back once more to their childhood's hero, Dr. Joe Bell, although Maitland is not a portrait of him but rather the outcome of a germinal idea. That very remoteness of Maitland, which roused criticism,[1] possessed charm for some readers, and he is the perfect foil for Alex Hope whom all reviewers applauded.

She is, even at the beginning of the book, the most mature in character of the Findlaters' heroines. She is the reverse of remote, with her sharp tongue and, on occasion, quick temper, her wit, her charming voice, her magnificent hair, her easy stride. Maitland compares her to a spray of flowering gorse which 'pricks but is sweet'. Despite lack of conventional good looks, Alex might have adorned any society, but her circumstances and her high sense of duty made her a household drudge and breadwinner in one. It is a hard and often a losing battle against poverty, yet she never allows herself to go under for long. The sober but not unhappy ending of the novel owes its brightness to her personality even more than to the vista of attractive possibility which opens before her. It is not the sound of marriage bells but a handsome little legacy which brings this good prospect into view. What, indeed, could be better in the human lot, given a sound character and stable disposition, than the fate of Alex Hope as she sails off towards a new world with her father for companion?

Wit and humour are delicate flowers; the puff of winds from a new age or a different climate fade and wither them rapidly. Doubtless Alex is not quite so sparkling now as she was to contemporary readers, but she is amusing still, as in her account of Miss Bessie Reed's going-away hat which had in it 'everything except a fox's brush – and I wasn't very sure about that!'[2] or her comments to herself upon the other women in the 'evilly ugly' station waiting-room at King's Cross and again when they are driving out to dine one cold evening, gliding swiftly over the smooth road, through pale fields and hedgerows with distant hills 'visible like milky-white shadows'

[1] *Spectator*, 18th April, p. 624.
[2] Mary and Jane Findlater, op. cit p. 196.

'There's a strange kind of gaiety about a night like this, isn't there?' said Alex. 'Like the pleasures of the Elysian fields. Couldn't you fancy the shades of the dead meeting for bodiless enjoyment by the light of the moon on such a frosty night as this? All of us, a troop of ghosts, just meeting in these well-known fields. Oh, I can imagine it perfectly – the queer, shimmering light and the frosty air – all the talk a little thin, none of us palpaple, and everything in greys and whites – and the way our eyes would glimmer!'[1]

The 'awareness' of Alex is far more acute than that of other characters in the book, with the exception, within limits peculiar to themselves, of Van Casalis and Robert Maitland. Her own spot of blindness is evident in her refusal to regard the 'unsuitable' Van Casalis with anything other than motherly affection. Marrying was still, in those days, the only recognized 'career' for a woman, and yet again, the Findlaters are insisting upon their question, 'What can the future hold for a single woman without means?' If her gifts fall short of genius, if she cannot bring herself to marry for the sake of a home, the brightest career is probably that of an aunt surrounded by young people in a family really needing her, otherwise there is the more likely fate of some grim, or vapid, soul-destroying form of domestic drudgery.

The novel is full of vividly alive and entertaining characters more lightly sketched in. 'Old Hopeful', Alex's father, is not only the incorrigible optimist and philanthropist that most of us have met in life and in books, he is also the period piece of a special date, for he is one of the nobler Vegetarians of the early 'Patent Food' years. It is a character compounded of high-mindedness and absurdity.

'You don't yet begin to understand his simple, noble nature,' declared Maitland to Alex. 'You have got all the common, everyday ideas that the world works with, and the sooner you unlearn then the better . . .'[2]

[1] Ibid., pp. 221–22.
[2] Ibid., p. 111.

but at least Alex has learnt to tolerate and be amused.

'Father,' she explains to another friend, 'is always bringing new
people to the house, trying new experiments in diet. I used to
think it dreadful ... but now I have come to see that it makes
life more lively ...'

Bringing home a family of Polish Jews to be housed and fed
was, of course, a more serious matter[1] than the helpings of 'nut-
tose' or 'gluttose' which were pressed upon unwilling or sceptical
guests, who would wash the nauseous stuff down with a hurried
gulp of wine, or be helped, surreptitiously by their hostess, to
dispose otherwise of the unwanted viands. To his children, who
could regard the food vagaries with a certain amount of amusement or indifference, listening tolerantly to his praise of 'that
beautiful marine creature' the cod, his theories of dress were more
embarrassing. He went to Edinburgh one morning wearing the
'single light garment', which he advocated, of blue woollen stuff,
'dyed and woven and made at home'. This, according to Alex,
was no laughing matter.[2]

His concern for the outcast or helpless, whether human or
animal, was matched by an apparent callousness which extended
to himself and his own comforts. His head was in the clouds and
the classics, his courage was magnificent. A far from unjustified
exclamation of despair from his daughter rouses him,

... 'The end of effort, Alex!' he cried, sitting forward in his
chair, and grasping the arms with his knobbly old hands. 'The
end of effort! Never ... what *is* our life but effort – effort and
energy ...'[3]

No character in the book is more forcefully drawn than Dolly
Orranmore. She is a shell of healthy animality, animality that is,
in its lowering sense. This, to the Findlaters, is nothing negative,
it is positively evil, and is portrayed by them in a manner both
subtle and horrifying, which makes this young woman one of

[1] Ibid., p. 4.
[2] Ibid., p. 79.
[3] Ibid., p. 342.

their most impressive achievements. She might be own cousin to the *Real Charlotte*,[1] except that even at this level of kinship, two such in one family would surely be mutually annihilating! In *Crossriggs*, or, for that matter, in almost any Findlater book, this power of darkness would be allowed no more than temporary and limited triumph.

There is one single telling adjective in which the peculiar individuality of this young woman is conveyed immediately, but in the main the effect is achieved cumulatively with one, often comparatively slight, incident after another, with a glance here from her 'large, shallow-set eyes'[2] or an echo there of her laughter.[3] The impression of those 'smooth, plump shoulders', her bare 'polished arms', the thick neck, the low cut, deep green evening gown, less a garment than a sheath from which the wearer was emerging, or rather bursting, her fine complexion, her give-away 'common little features', the small, thick, white strong hands, the carnation scent diffusing itself from her skirts as she walked,[4] are all strokes of the pen, significant to a certain degree in themselves, but incomparably more so in relation to each other and to the completed portrait.

Her lack of physical fear and of some of the perhaps rather endearing feminine frailties and traits[5] brought out in the little scene when she intervenes to scatter the young bullocks from Alex's path, the 'spring and finish in her every movement, suggestive of superabundant vitality'[6], emphasize by contrast the rottenness within. She has little or no response to anything but the purely material. In the face of tragedy and human sorrow, she collapses and shrinks away. 'I can do nothing' is all she has to say. She is one of those beings who assails the integrity of the very souls of others.

Much of this effect is gained from the instinctive shrinking of Alex on several occasions from something alien or repugnant

[1] Heroine of the book of that name by Edith Œnone Somerville and Martin Ross.

[2] Mary and Jane Findlater, op. cit.   [3] pp. 188, 230.

[4] p. 225.   [5] Ibid., p. 264.   [6] Ibid., p. 225.

which is half-seen, half-sensed, and leaves an unpleasant aftermath of perturbation in the mind. But Alex was too perceptive not to be more than dimly and uncomfortably aware, and her answer to Mathilda's question about the admiral's dinner-party contains the telling word. Referring to the Orranmores, Mathilda asks her sister,

'What are they like?'

and Alex replies,

> 'Like? Oh, the man is like the rind of something squeezed – no use at all to anyone, I should think, and the woman is like a Harpy in a wig – and the girl . . .'
> 'Well?' said Mathilda.
> Alex looked at her affectionately as she sat on the fender holding up one hand to screen her face from the fire.
> 'Oh, Mathilda,' she exclaimed, 'with all your faults you're a nice creature, so good, so *chaste*.'[1]

Scarcely less significant is Robert Maitland's reaction at this same party, when he looks across at Miss Orranmore, once, twice and then, 'with an almost imperceptible movement, slight, but final – as an animal turns away its head from the hand of a stranger – he turned away to address himself to Miss Brinley'.[2]

Upon Miss Brinley and Miss Maitland, who had nothing in common except that they were ladies of the old school, Miss Orranmore could have but one effect. To them she was plainly a wanton, outraging every respectable convention and standard of womanly behaviour. Through their reactions the portrait is deftly tinted and shaded off into comedy.

However lightly sketched, there is scarcely a person mentioned who is not made real and alive. None is more so in this book than Miss Bessie Reid, who lives with an old, partially paralysed aunt 'making a brave effort' as the neighbours said of her, wearing buckles, bangles, rings and showy ill-made clothes, to keep up her courage, always affectionate and perfectly satisfied with her

[1] Ibid., p. 236. The italics are mine. E.K.M.
[2] Ibid., p. 227.

unexpected and unlikely romance in the form of the 'cultured', chinless botanist, Mr. Massie, with an Adam's apple in his throat that 'worked up and down so convulsively that she [Alex] longed to say, "Oh, do make an effort and swallow it for once!"'[1]

Mathilda is an almost complete foil for Alex, her sister, but she possesses nearly all the right instincts, together with a wonderful placidity and not a little obtuseness. She is perfectly contented to end her widowhood, comfort the rejected suitor of Alex and become Mrs. James Reid, to live 'happily ever after' in the cheerful dullness of Eastshire.

'The children', Alex's nephews and nieces, in their minor way are individuals, and the novel contains many more, including the maids, and especially among these Katharine, whose rejection of much needed help is characteristic,

An ominous silence; then Katharine began in a low recitation – 'Get yer girl, mem – oh, yes, get yer girl – trauchlin' through the house making more work than she's worth, eating her head off, dirtying plates, and carrying gossip, and her in earrings, likely, and sayin' we can't get through with our own work, and me done every blessed thing in this house, miss, forbye Mr. Hope's food – that's a woman's work itself when spinach and all that has to be prepared. Oh, get yer girl! I know what the end will be!'[2]

The book is far more than a collection of characters, although the story has its foundation in them. It is a record, in the main, of small things. Intimate sorrows and joys are made real and moving through the people concerned. There is only one happening on the larger and tragic scale. Generally speaking, this is what village life amounts to usually. The novel has unity and concentration through its strong, underlying intention, but an attempt to abstract this intention would give a quite falsely didactic impression. It is intended to represent life in a small community as truly as the writers were able to depict it and this

[1] Ibid., p. 179.
[2] Ibid., p. 28.

novel shows at its best the Findlaters' skill in depicting such a community and in living characterization. In these terms they find the human lot, on balance, worth while, perpetually interesting, basically good. Despite the perversity and disappointment inherent in mortal stuff and material existence, despite cross-grained circumstance, for the courageous spirit enough in love with life for its own sake, the rewards are almost unfailing, be they in unfamiliar guise or to be found on unexpected levels.

As a work of art *Penny Monypenny* represents, in the main, no advance upon *Crossriggs*. It is less concentrated because it lacks unity of place, nor does it possess a heroine as dominating as Alex. Yet the virtues of the book lie within the time-honoured domain of romantic narrative and the story is endowed with an added depth and charm through the sensitive delineation of its northern setting. This is not obtruded, it mingles with the narrative, but the note is authentic and vibrant with beauty, especially for those who know Scotland. The story moves between the Highlands and the Lowlands, as the Findlaters themselves had gone from one to the other. Nor is there any loss of skill in characterization, rather the contrary.

Lorin Weir in *Penny Monypenny* is a considerably more developed version of Van Casalis of *Crossriggs*, with marked differences. He belongs to a type which appears from time to time in the sisters' novels. Darnley Stair in Mary's *The Rose of Joy*, Michael Fletcher in Jane's *Rachel*, Herman in her *Ladder to the Stars* all belong to the same tribe, while not unrelated is Voinovitch in Mary's *Tents of a Night*. These possess something temperamental in common and are, in varying degree, alien and unhappy in their surroundings. They are dark complexioned, 'dark strangers' except for Darnley Stair, who is sallow and red-haired, but none the less, possesses many of the 'family' characteristics. This type is not 'lucky' in the Findlaters' books and the 'dark strangers' are almost inevitably tragic persons for them. Broadly they are alike, but in detail, very different. Darnley Stair has little in common with any of the group, except Lorin Weir. Lorin and Van who are more alike, are yet contrasted. Van possesses youthful health and beauty, Lorin is delicate, precocious with thin stooped shoulders and a sardonic humour which is accentuated with the years. Of the Auntly type there are several notable figures in *Penny Monypenny* though it is 'Cousin Isabella' the 'hoodie craw' who carries the honours as Aunt Rampant of the story.

The plot of *Penny Monypenny* (another Borthwick family true story) turns upon the extinction of a branch of the Monypennys at the house of Tullyvee in Fifeshire. The old people are portrayed with exquisite verisimilitude, 'their hard Scotch faces . . . etched with lines not altogether mean lines, but made narrow by a narrow life and deep feelings', even the Tullyvee dogs, with their 'broad paws and waddling gait' possessed the family traits and 'found a certain melancholy satisfaction in a funeral'.

Something of the atmosphere of the Scottish landscape enters the very mood of the writers themselves both here and in other books, but especially here. It is a climate, so far as one can generalize about it, where winter is long and tough, summer and autumn brief, but with their incomparable moments of flaming or serene glory. Beauty tends to be as fragile as the hare-bell (the native bluebell) or remote and austere. Human beings cannot easily take liberties with nature. There is a matter of fact inevitability about the consequences and little human lives are circumscribed prosaically enough, though on the edge of the confines always lies, thinly veiled, the possibility of ecstasy or despair, the one revealed, maybe, by an exquisite summer morning, the other by a strange, dark crag.

Beneath the Visiting Moon is composed of two parts, the first of which was concerned with the fortunes, or rather misfortunes of a young, beautiful rather empty-headed little governess, the second with the happier fate of her daughter. The destiny of these two is intertwined with the lives of a triangle of families; first, the Shores of a remote Devon rectory, not insensitive or unresponsive to the newer ways of the world, but quite unassailable in a supremely English way. Next there are the Blacks of 'Black's Blacking', installed at Rothsay Terrace, Edinburgh. They are in process of climbing a social scale which crosses that down which an ancient Scottish family, the Mauchlynes, are rapidly sliding, through degeneracy to ruin. Moth-eaten pride and squalid environment are depicted with unsparing veracity.

Beneath the Visiting Moon is not quite like any of the Findlaters' other books. The shadows are more sharply defined and are, in a sense, more sinister and unpleasant. The rotten existence of the ne'er do well, Steenie Mauchlyne, takes its sordid course through both parts. But the highlights of the book, although it is down to earth in the characteristically Findlater manner, have an other worldly quality. The Shore ladies possess a kind of luminosity which may owe something to the writers' beloved friend, Victoria Cholmondeley, while her father may well have suggested old Mr. Shore.

Here also the Findlaters' interest is manifest in that phenomenon of earlier twentieth-century decades, 'the modern girl', whom Mary had already depicted with sympathy in *Tents of a Night* (1914) and who, as Tib Grant, is introduced in Part I of *Beneath the Visiting Moon* as the eight-year-old charge of the young governess, and as the medical student in Part II.

The winds of change are persistently present in this story, but the Findlaters could not convey their reaction to and passionate interest in the new ways of the world through a different medium. In so far as they possessed the new wine, it would have to be poured into old bottles. The critics, who by 1923 had slipped into the habit of bowing and smiling the sisters' books into the homes of a welcoming public, praised as loudly as ever, perhaps more loudly than before. At the same time an under-current of something else here and there revealed itself. A few strictures in *The Times Literary Supplement* (3rd May, 1923) blew counter to its large gusts of adulation. The general trend of dissatisfaction was thus summed up: 'Romancing is not quite exigent enough.'

The Findlaters' art was beginning to look old-fashioned. Novels more analytical, more form conscious and concentrated were required. On the upper levels of the art, Henry James and Virginia Woolf were setting the tone. On the lower, the pink sugar of O. Douglas was preferred to the Findlaters' stringency.

As to an estimate of the sisters' literary achievement, its significance is perhaps pointed by Raymond Mortimer's comment when he reviewed *Beneath the Visiting Moon* in *The New Statesman*. He saw a real function for this, the Findlaters' last novel, in continuing the Victorian tradition both of writing for the public and writing well, to supply those who could not yet 'in this generation' get much from Virginia Woolf or D. H. Lawrence.[1]

If one is affixing such labels, the Findlaters were assuredly 'Victorians' in most senses, and this marks them off from Susan Ferrier, who has more affinities with the eighteenth century and who knew English society mainly at second hand. Yet the sisters' literary lineage is nearest to Miss Ferrier, though their books were not 'directly descended'. Obviously Mary's and Jane's novels are not of the 'kailyard' any more than of the 'pink sugar' school. Their writings have neither that pungency of dialect nor ultra sweetness of sentiment. Brutality was as little in their natures as in their lives, so that for them it could never be a road to realism. They did not totally ignore or shun it, but they never pursued their stories on the level of *The House with the Green Shutters*,[2] Their world, like that of Jane Austen's novels, was a 'ladies' world', one which, after all, constitutes a considerable part of civilized life, nor in its own way, unless the whole world reverts to savagery, is it necessarily so far from reality or so ephemeral as some would have us believe.

The Findlaters were forgotten by subsequent generations and their books are now unread. In their day, Mary and Jane depicted faithfully the life they knew and a wide range of very different readers, 'high, low and middle-brow' loved their stories. Whether any of their books transcended their age it is too soon to pronounce with certainty, but there can be no doubt that they illuminate a facet of their world as in their time.

---

[1] *The New Statesman,* 12th May, 1923, pp. 145–46.

[2] George Douglas (Brown) *The House with the Green Shutters,* 1901.

Books

MARY

1895. *Songs & Sonnets.*

1897. *Over the Hills.*
1899. *Betty Musgrave.*
1901. *A Narrow Way.*
1903. *The Rose of Joy.*
1907. *A Blind Bird's Nest.*
1914. *Tents of a Night.*

JANE

1896. *The Green Graves of Balgowrie.*
1897. *A Daughter of Strife.*
1899. *Rachel.*
1902. *The Story of a Mother.*
1904. *Stones from a Glass House.*
1905. *All that Happened in a Week.*
1906. *The Ladder to the Stars.*
1912. *Seven Scots Stories.*
1921. *A Green Grass Widow and Other Stories.*

MARY and JANE

1908. *Crossriggs.*
1911. *Penny Monypenny.*
1916. *Content With Flies.*
1923. *Beneath the Visiting Moon.*

1901. *Tales that are Told.*

1916. *Seen and Heard Before and After 1914.*

1904. With Kate Douglas Wiggin and Allan McAulay. *The Affair at the Inn.*

1911. With Kate Douglas Wiggin and Allan McAulay. *Robinetta.*

Index

Abercrombie, Dr. John, 118
Ardvorlich, 17–18, 24, 26, 84, 107, 120
Arkansas, 65, 72

Bacon, Selden and Josephine, 50–51
Balfour, Lady Frances, 35–36, 98
Balnakiel, 1–2
Beer, 42, 52
Blaikie, Margaret, 49
Bell, Dr. Joseph, 21–22, 91, 136
Borthwick Family, 2–3, 19–20, 27, 33, 38, 46–47, 130
Borthwick, Jane (Aunt), 19–20, 22, 34, 36, 55, 92
    Hymns from The Land of Luther, 20
    Journals of, 92–93
Borthwick, Margaret (Aunt), 47–48
Boston, 54–59, 62
    parties in, 56–58
Bunder (Findlaters' maid), 100–1, 111, 120–1
    death of, 121
Burnett, Mrs. Frances Hodgson, 51–52

Cadell, Marion, xiii, 14, 20, 29, 93, 100, 103, 111, 113–15, 119, 122–4
    family of, 29, 35, 92, 100
Cambridge, U.S.A., 59, 65
Carnegie, Mr. and Mrs. Andrew, 53, 78
Cholmondeley, Mary and Victoria, 84–89, 93–94, 98, 112–13, 121, 144

Cholmondeley, Diana, 86–87
    father of, 87–88, 144
Christian Science, 55
Clover Bend, 65, 68–72
Cockenzie xiii, 29, 84, 100–1
Comrie, 123, 125
Corbet, Mr. and Mrs. Rowland, 90, 121
Crawford, Dowager Countess of, 84
    Lindsay, Lady Mabel and Lady Jane, 84–85
Crawford, Mrs., 68, 70–71
Creighton, Louise, 82
Cunningham, Miss, 29

De La Mare, Walter, 90–91, 117
Deland, Margaret, 51
Drake, Mr. (plantation manager), 68–71
Durness, 1–2, 45, 47

Edenchip, 5, 15, 24, 124
Edinburgh, 1–2, 4, 17–19, 22, 27–28, 34–35, 37–38, 84, 130, 138
Embleton, 38, 42
Emerson, Miss Ellen, 60–61
Emerson, Ralph Waldo, 60, 63, 89

Fallodon, 38–39, 41–42, 80, 82, 109
Findlater, Rev. Eric (father), xii, 1, 3–4, 9, 11–14, 25–26, 28, 45–47
    marriage, 3;
    sisters of, 20;
    death of, 25–26
Findlater Family, 19, 24, 130

FINDLATER, JANE HELEN and MARY WILLIAMINA, xi–xiii *et seq.*
childhood 1–26; parents and aunts, 2–4, 19–22; education, 10–11, 17; beauty, 14, 23; poverty, 28, 33; change of fortunes, 34; American tour, xiii, 49–78; friends old and new, 79–98, 101–2, 105–7, 121, 123–5; war work, 99–100, 105–6; illness of Mary, 115; Paignton, Torquay, Rye, Comrie (life at), q.v.; B.B.C. talk by Jane, 120; illness and death of Jane, 124–5;

DIARIES and LETTERS: xii–xiii, 20, 29, 33–35, 50–59, 61, 63, 66–78, 84, 93, 100, 103–5, 108, 111–15, 119, 122–4, 130;

BOOKS (for chronology see p. 146), 128–46; characters in, 130–44; qualities of, 129–45;

(by JANE)
All that Happened in a Week, 146; *Allan Grey: An Indigent Gentlewoman,* 33; *A Daughter of Strife,* 146; *A Green Grass Widow and Other Stories,* 128, 146; *The Green Graves of Balgowrie,* xi, 33–37, 80, 128, 130–2, 146; *The Ladder to the Stars,* 79, 83, 142, 146; *Rachel,* 80, 128, 132–3, 146; *Seven Scotch Stories,* 68, 128, 146; (including *Charlie over the Water,* 68;) *Stones from a Glass House,* 128, 146; *The Story of a Mother,* 42, 86, 146;

(by MARY)
Betty Musgrave, 42, 146; *A Blind Bird's Nest,* 83, 146; *A Narrow Way,* 20, 34, 146; *Over the Hills,* 146; *The Rose of Joy,* 27, 60, 74–75, 79, 128, 133, 142, 146; *Songs and Sonnets,* 10, 128, 146; *Tents of a Night,* 79, 142, 144, 146;

(by JANE and MARY)
Beneath the Visiting Moon, xi, 109, 114–15, 128–9, 143–6; *Content with Flies,* 99, 128, 146; *Crossriggs,* 85, 92, 97, 128–9, 134–43, 146; *Penny Monypenny,* 8, 16, 97, 99, 128–9, 142–3, 146; *Seen and Heard Before and After 1914,* 103, 128, 146; *Tales that are Told,* 128, 146;

(with KATE DOUGLAS WIGGIN and ALLAN MCAULAY)
The Affair at the Inn, 128, 146; *Robinetta,* 128, 146

Findlater, Jessie (aunt), 9, 14, 21
Findlater, Mora (Sarah Jemima), 4, 8, 14–15, 21–22, 24, 27, 31, 34, 37–38, 53, 86, 99, 116
illness and recovery, 37–38; protégée (Maggie Taylor), 53; death of, 120
Findlater, Robina, (aunt), 20, 56
Findlater, Mrs. née Sarah Laurie Borthwick (mother), 2–4, 9–11, 18, 22–23, 25, 27–29, 31–33, 36, 39, 42–43, 46, 86, 130
marriage, 3, 46; sisters of, 4, 9, 19–20; death of, 86
Findlater, Rev. William and Mrs., (grandparents), 1–2, 45
family of, 2
Finlay, William (great grandfather), 97
French, Miss Alice (Octave Thanet), 65–66, 68–71, 73
Furse, Henry, 93

Gladstone, Rt. Hon. W. E., xi, 36
Gladstone, Miss Constance, 36
Glenconner, Lady, Pamela (afterwards Viscountess Grey of Fallodon), 89, 99, 106–7, 110
children of, 106–7; second marriage (1921), 110; spiritualistic experiences, 106–7

Gray Family, 22–25, 49, 89

Grey, Lady (Dorothy), née
    Widdrington, 14, 38–42, 45–46,
    80–85, 100
    marriage, 40; death, 80–81

Grey of Fallodon, Viscount (Sir
    Edward Grey), 40–42, 80–83,
    85, 106, 109–10, 121
    first and second marriages, 40, 89
    letters of, 82–83, 109–10

Haldane, Richard Burdon, M.P., 35,
    95 (later Viscount Haldane)

Hawthorne, Nathaniel, 64

Heber, Bishop, 88

Higginson, Col. Thomas Went-
    worth, 57

Hill, Margaret, afterwards Roberton
    (q.v.)

Hill, Rev. Thomas, and Mrs., 7

Hitchcock Family, 75–76

Houghton, Mr. and Mrs., 62–63

Howe, Mrs. Julia Ward, 58

Howells, William Dean, 66, 77
    daughter of, 77

Hoxie, 66–68, 72

Inge, Dean, 90, 121

Itchen, 41

Jacob, Violet, 98–99

James, Henry, xi, 54, 62–63, 77–79,
    94–97, 100–1, 103–4, 111
    death of, 103

James, William and Alice, 57, 59–62,
    79–80, 84–85, 94–95, 97, 103–5,
    family of, 94–95, 103–4

Jones, Sir Lawrence, 103, 105
    marriage, 105

Kemp, Agnes and Alice, 95, 103, 105,
    108

Kipling, Mr. and Mrs. Rudyard, 38,
    43, 99, 115

Lang, The Most Rev. Cosmo,
    Archbishop of Canterbury, xi

Lawrence, D. H., 145

Lochearnhead, 1–27, 88, 92, 107, 123,
    125, 129

London, 32, 45, 80–82, 84, 92, 101,
    105

Lorrain Smith, Miss Annie, (gover-
    ness) 10–11

McAulay, Allan (see Stewart, Char-
    lotte), 128, 146

Macgillivray, Alexander and Mrs., 3,
    11–12, 33, 99

Macgregor, Lady Helen, 5, 24
    children of, 24

Macgregor, Very Rev. William, 38,
    103

Maclagan, Mary and family, 31, 123,
    125

Marham Church, Cornwall, 36–37

Memphis (Tennessee), 73–74

Minor, Dr. and Mrs., 73–74

Moncrieff, Georgina, 33

Netherhampton, 93

New York, 50–54, 65, 76–77, 97

Newbolt, Sir Henry and Lady, 80, 90,
    93, 110

Norton, Professor Charles and Mrs.,
    59–60
    Norton, Miss Sally, 60

Paignton, 42–43, 92, 99, 101, 105,
    108, 112–15, 116

Perkins, Miss Jane, 56

Pfeiffer Family, 89–90

Piper, Mrs. (medium), 62

Polmont, 97

Prestonpans, 27–48

Reay, Lord, 47

Reiss Family, 90

Riggs, Kate, née Smith (see also
    Wiggin), 44, 49–51, 54, 65, 84,
    111–12, 128, 146
    friends of, 50–51, 65;

INDEX

Riggs—*Continued*
  parties, 50–51;
  Riggs, George, 50
Roberton, Mrs. (née Margaret Hill),
  6–8, 17, 57, 85–86, 92, 102, 123;
  family of, 6–7
Robertson, Miss Jane (governess), 15
Rye, 103, 109–10, 112, 115–23
  friends in, 119

Salem, 63–65
Schuster family, 89–91
Schuster, Paula (afterwards Lady
  Jones), 89–91, 101, 103, 105
  marriage, 105
Scotland, xii, 2, 32, 45, 92, 112
Seton, Mr. and Mrs. Thompson,
  52–53
Smalley, Mrs. and Miss, 65, 76–78
Somerset, Lady Henry, 106
Sprott, Miss, 29–31, 35
  nieces of, 30, 35
Stewart, Charlotte, (Allan McAulay),
  17–18, 27, 32–33, 44, 84–85, 105,
  107, 109, 128

mother of, 18, 21, 24, 85, 107, 120
  death of, 107, 109
Sutherland, Millicent, Duchess of, 45
Terry, Ellen, xi, 36–37, 101–2, 112
  letters from, 37
Torquay, 43–46, 49, 84, 86, 92, 103,
  116
Tucker, Colonel, 68–70
Tuke, Sir John Batty, 38

Venice, 84–85
Vulliamy, Miss, 44

Washington, 75–76
de Watteville, Walter, 22
Wemyss, Countess of, 35
Wick, 7, 84, 92
Wiggin, Kate Douglas (*see also*
  Riggs), 128, 146
Woolf, Virginia, 116–17, 145
World War I, 79, 98–108, 113
World War II, 123–4

Yeats, Jack, 43
Yeats, W. B., 43, 54